From the same author:

"La Rentabilite des Investissements, Analyse du risque et strategies", *Presses Universitaires de France.*

INVESTMENTS PROFITABILITY, TIME VALUE & RISK ANALYSIS

GUIDELINES FOR INDIVIDUALS AND CORPORATIONS

Eric Matter

PARTRIDGE

Copyright © 2019 by Eric Matter.

ISBN:	Hardcover	978-1-5437-5182-6
	Softcover	978-1-5437-5180-2
	eBook	978-1-5437-5181-9

All rights reserved. No part of this book may be used or reproduced by any means, graphic, electronic, or mechanical, including photocopying, recording, taping or by any information storage retrieval system without the written permission of the author except in the case of brief quotations embodied in critical articles and reviews.

Because of the dynamic nature of the Internet, any web addresses or links contained in this book may have changed since publication and may no longer be valid. The views expressed in this work are solely those of the author and do not necessarily reflect the views of the publisher, and the publisher hereby disclaims any responsibility for them.

Print information available on the last page.

To order additional copies of this book, contact
Toll Free 800 101 2657 (Singapore)
Toll Free 1 800 81 7340 (Malaysia)
orders.singapore@partridgepublishing.com

www.partridgepublishing.com/singapore

CONTENTS

Introduction vii

Chapter 1   Basic Financial Concepts 1
Chapter 2   Time Value and Discounting 17
Chapter 3   Profitability Criteria 29
Chapter 4   Influence of External Financing and Inflation 45
Chapter 5   Risk Analysis and Evaluation in Un-Certain Future 55
Chapter 6   Application to Practical Cases - Simulations 85
Chapter 7   Profitability of Public Investments 101

Appendix 1   Dedicated Companion Web Site 111
Appendix 2   Summary of Useful Formulas 117
Bibliography 119

INTRODUCTION

Shall we buy a property on own funds, or rather borrow and invest our cash resources on stock market?

Is it more cost-effective to own a car or lease it out?

Shall a company upgrade its existing factory on equities, or scrap it and invest more in a new one through a financial loan?

Shall an Oil & Gas Operator monetize its natural gas production in generating power, or producing fertilizers?

Shall it select a high Capex / low Opex investment or the opposite?

How time is impacting the selection of an investment option?

What is the sensitivity of our selection to discount rate, inflation, loan rate, tax rate, and how do they interact with each other...?

What is the risk of selecting a wrong option?

We, Individuals and Corporations, are permanently facing critical choices in selecting the best options to optimize our own and limited resources, or sorting out how to maximize the profitability of our investments.

The economic and financial environment will participate our decision, through such parameters like financial markets outlook, external funds availability, interest rates, inflation, taxes policies...but a more subjective perception of TIME will still keep a key role in our global appreciation.

The profitability analysis methodology based on discounted cash-flows, as developed in this guide, can be applied to any kind of investment by corporations or individuals, and uses universal criteria allowing the selection of any form of investment or spending, with and without external financing.

It is explaining the central role and crucial effect of TIME in the appreciation of VALUE, and how it can affect the outcome of such analysis.

This guide provides then elements on methods to include risk and un-certain future in profitability analysis and investments selection.

Last, an introduction is made to public investments selection methodologies.

Its aim is to assist all participants (engineers, bankers, deciders…) to an investment evaluation, in using common concepts and a common language.

It is also meant to help and support the decision of individual buyers and consumers in their everyday life, and allow non-financial officers and students to better understand the criteria used by banks and financial institutions.

Detailed calculations and formulas have been minimized and focus is brought instead on the meaning of concepts, principles of analysis and methodologies of selection, with the help of several practical cases.

A dedicated and registered companion website (below link) is allowing an instant connection to a suite of spreadsheets detailing the simulation of study cases, through a financial model involving the key parameters.

The reader may use it to perform his own calculations and simulations, and to eventually improve it with the inclusion of other parameters or risk analysis.

https://www.investments-profitability-calculations-ericmatter.com

CHAPTER 1

BASIC FINANCIAL CONCEPTS

1.1 Income Statement 1
1.2 Investment 2
1.3 Depreciation 4
1.4 Financial interests 5
    1.4.1 Actuarial rate 5
    1.4.2 Repayment modes 6
    1.4.3 Capitalized interests 8
1.5 Working capital 10
    1.5.1 Definition 10
    1.5.2 Financing of the working capital 11
1.6 Taxes 12
    1.6.1 VAT 12
    1.6.2 Income tax 12
    1.6.3 Other taxes and incentives 12
1.7 Inflation 13
    1.7.1 Analysis in current currency 13
    1.7.2 Analysis in constant currency 13

CHAPTER 1

Basic Financial Concepts

1.1 Income Statement

The Profit or Loss of a given production process basically derives from the following sequence :

- The Sales or Turnover is measuring the commercial activity during the Period.
- The total Production is obtained by adding/deducting the Inventory increase/decrease to the Sales during the period.
- The Added Value is obtained by deducting the cost of required raw materials, energy and transformation consumables from the Production.
- The EBITDA derives from the Added Value by further deducting the cost of corresponding salaries, wages, direct social burden and overheads (non productive staff and management).
- The Net Profit is then obtained by deducting from EBITDA the provision for assets depreciation, the financing interests, the dividends to shareholders, and the income tax.

It is to note that the ratio EBITDA/Investment is a good reference indicator of the intrinsic profitability of an Investment, while the Net profit takes into account the fiscal environment and company corporate policies.

From the above accounting terms, we will derive practical and common terms and concepts for the elaboration of financial analysis :

- Operations Costs will consist in variable costs (materials and energy) and fixed costs (direct and un-direct), such as labor, various taxes, insurances, overheads, maintenance...)
- Production Costs will be the sum of Operation Costs, depreciation and Financing Interests.
- Profit before Tax will be obtained by deducting Production Costs from Sales.
- Net Profit is then obtained after further deduction of income tax.

The "Cash-Flow" is the algebraic addition of Net Profit + Provision for depreciation + other provisions + Assets disposal capital gains – Assets disposal capital losses +/- Variation of the need in working capital (see 1.5.2 below).

It is an essential criterion used in profitability analysis, that measures the sustainable solvency and the ability of a productive investment to continuously finance its growth and remunerate the investors.

1.2 Investment

The investment is the primary step necessary to initiate any economic or industrial activity.

The validation of a Corporate investment lies on :

1. Its relevance to the market, or the assessment of the market it will create.
2. The selection of the technology that its implementation is based on.
3. The estimation of the required Cap(ital) and Op(eration) ex(penditures).
4. The evaluation of the profitability of the capital invested
5. The identification, evaluation and mitigation of the risks at all stages of the analysis.

The marketing analysis, first step of above sequence, is pre-requisite to any investment analysis.

The second and third steps are integrated into a global optimization of the selected technology and the capital to mobilize.

A productive investment shall meet the market performance expectations, and lead to the minimum Capex and Opex.

However, It is exposed to technology reliability, design & construction contingencies, operation risks and environmental liabilities, therefore Capex/Opex will be subject to adequate contingencies.

This guide is providing standard guidelines for the evaluation of the profitability of a given investment, assuming it fits the market.

An investment is a "cashed-out" cash-flow that is supposed to generate further "cashed-in" cash-flows through the planned activity.

It can be spread over several years, oftentimes on an S-curve time distribution, and be constituted of such phases as studies, design, procurement, construction, commissioning and start-up.

An industrial investment is generally split into 2 main portions :

- The "local" portion, made of local materials and construction purchased in local currency, on equity or financed through local banks.
- The "foreign" portion, materialized by special studies or equipment procured abroad on foreign currencies, generally financed through export credits or soft loans.

This split is subject to optimization of the financing and taxation schemes.

1.3 Depreciation

Any investment or tangible asset is subject to a depreciation, which is the accounting acknowledgement of a loss of value in time.

This loss of value is due to its usage or its obsolescence while technology is evolving.

It is a provision made from the EBITDA for the purpose of asset future replacement, which is not actually cashed out, but taken into account in the fiscal calculation of the net profit.

It is part of the cash-flow generated from the investment, and the investor remains actually free to use it for its primary purpose (wise replacement of an asset), or re-allocate it, temporarily or not, for another purpose.

An asset has oftentimes an actual lifetime longer than its accounting depreciation. At the end of the reference period of an economic or profitability study (for instance 20 years) it carries then a residual value.

This residual value is considered as "scrap value" when the asset is decommissioned and not producing any longer.

If the asset can be subject to life extension for further use or production, its residual value will depend on the market, or valued from its ability to still generate cash-flow (for instance 5 years of cash-flow).

If the residual value is greater than the initial investment, it is then considered as an appreciation or capital gain, and become subject to a specific tax upon cession.

This situation can be met in the case of a building dedicated to rental activity : despite its accounting depreciation, its residual value may have appreciated after the rental period of reference.

The mode of depreciation is usually "linear", ie spread in equal amounts over the period (for instance 20 years for a building, 10 years for machinery, 5 years for cars, 2 years for computing equipment…).

It may also be decreasing along the time, for instance with the "double declining balance" method, whereby the depreciation of the net accounting balance is twice the linear amount.

1.4 Financial interests

In the case of a financing, the profitability study becomes a global and simultaneous analysis of the project and its financing.

However, the resulting profitability criteria are provided with and without financing, to allow the lending entity to appreciate the viability of the project itself, which in return will constitute a guarantee that the investor will be able to repay the loan(s).

To know the specific profitability of the project alone will also allow the investor to evaluate the impact of increasing or decreasing the loan amount, depending on its features :

- Rate
- Total repayment period
- Grace period
- Repayment mode
- Repayment terms frequency
- Insurance cost (specific rate to add to the loan rate) and administration cost.

1.4.1 Actuarial rate

A loan can be studied as a project in itself, and its internal rate of return (IRR) (*) can be calculated from the borrower standpoint, or from the investor standpoint (for instance an investment in a bond).

This particular IRR is the actuarial rate of the loan (or bond investment).

It is the "discount rate" (*) at which the algebraic sum of the discounted cash-flows resulting from the loan (or from the bond investment) along the reference period is zero.

In other words, it is the discount rate at which cashed-in loan amount is balanced with the discounted cashed-out repayments, or the discount rate at which cashed-out bond investment is balanced with the discounted cashed-in revenues.

It can be adjusted by any taxation rate, resulting from a given tax regulation.

If "i" is the taxation rate and "j" is the loan rate, then the net actuarial rate is j*(1 – i)

It is a common criterion taking into account all expenses and revenues (insurances, ancillary costs, coupons.....), which will allow a comparison between different loans or bonds.

Application : Once the borrower gets the actuarial rate of a proposed loan, he will be then able to determine the eventual leverage procured by this loan to finance an investment having a certain IRR.

Basically, he will improve the economics of the investment by borrowing if the loan actuarial rate is lower than the investment IRR.

More generally, a loan will procure a financial advantage to the borrower if the loan's actuarial rate is lower than the current discount rate of the borrower's own funds.

It means that if both rates are equal, the algebraic sum of the loan's discounted cash flows is Zero.

(*) The concepts of IRR and discount rate will be developed in Chapter 2.

1.4.2 Repayment modes

→ The straight-line loan amortization, or constant capital amortization, is a method by which the capital is repaid by equal parts at each period, and the interests paid at each period apply on the remaining capital.

Installments amounts are therefore gradually decreasing along the repayment period.

Advantage : It leads to a quicker reduction of outstanding balance (compared to mortgages).

Disadvantage : It implies a heavier burden at the beginning, while the investment's income is still fragile, and is more difficult to manage for budgeting purposes, as the overall repayment amount is continuously changing over the time.

→ The mortgage amortization is a classic mode of loan amortization, widely used by banks for individuals in the financing of property acquisition.

The loan repayment amounts (capital + interests) remain the same along the period.
The part of repaid interests is bigger at the beginning and it takes therefore longer to reduce the capital balance.
The calculation is less simple but it offers more simplicity for budgeting purposes.

The following graphs are displaying the different situations.

For the sake of clarity, the relative proportion of interests vs capital is purposely exaggerated.

Document 1 - STRAIGHT LINE LOAN AMORTIZATION

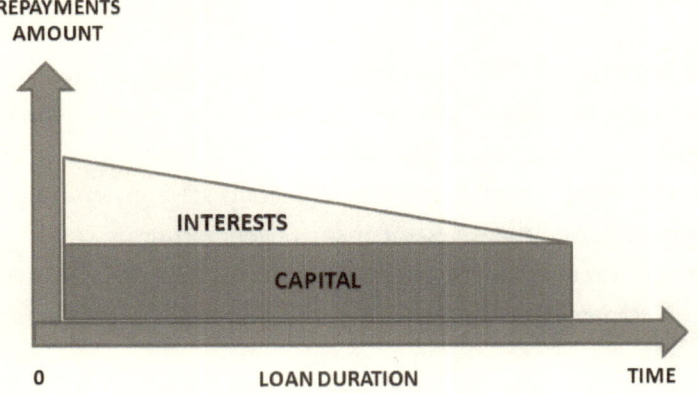

Document 2 - MORTGAGE LOAN AMORTIZATION

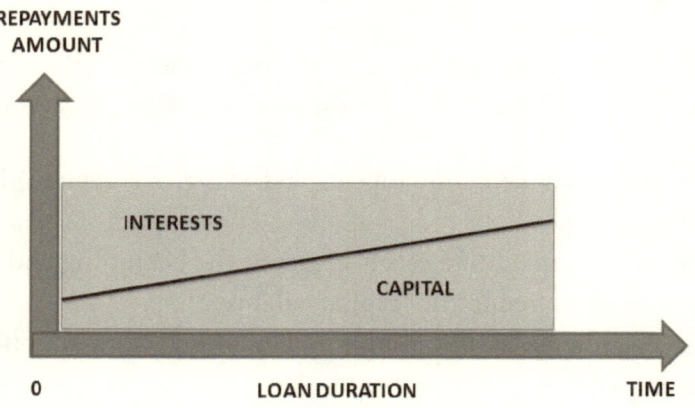

Note : The calculation of the sum of the discounted cash-flows for the 2 modes over the same period and with the same nominal interest rate shows that the mortgage mode is more detrimental to the borrower. The drawback of the mortgage will worsen while the loan duration will increase.

1.4.3 Capitalized interests

For industrial entities, the investment is generally not done as a single disbursement at "time 0", but through a development or construction period that may last years, typically over an "S" curve.

The borrowed capital (or loan) will then start generating interests to be repaid before the investment starts generating revenues.

These "interests during investemnt" are then to be added to the initial investment and are generally to be repaid on equities, as shown below.

Document 3 - INTERESTS DURING INVESTMENT PERIOD: PAID UPFRONT

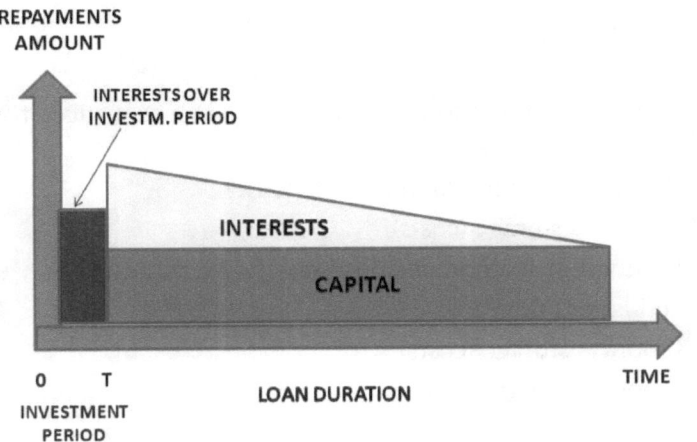

As such up-front interests may be a heavy burden, the investor may elect to "capitalize" them in the main loan, i.e. to add them to the "base load" capital, in such a way they can be repaid when revenues will be available.

These interests will themselves generate interests, as shown below.

This is a more onerous option, but this is also the price to pay to avoid disbursing up-front cash resources.

Document 4 - INTERESTS DURING INVESTMENT PERIOD: CAPITALIZED

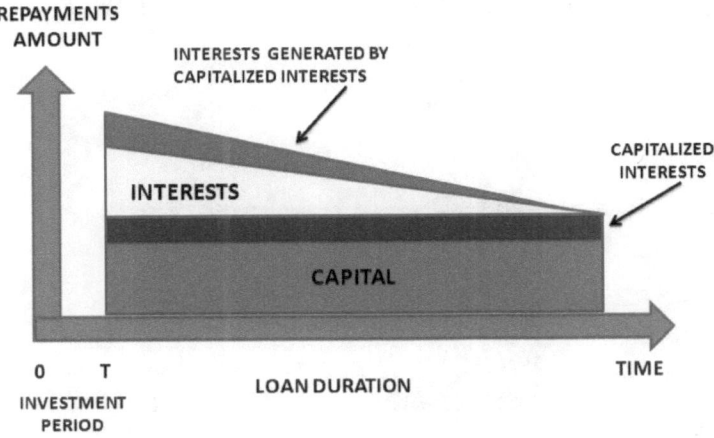

1.5 Working capital

1.5.1 Definition

An Industrial production process consists in a sequence of stages :

- Raw materials procurement (expense)
- Materials storage (costs)
- Production (equipment depreciation & maintenance, utilities and labor costs)
- Products storage (costs)
- Products sale (revenue)

These operations occur one after the other, and revenues generally take place after expenses are paid.

This requires a permanent - and eventually variable - excess of cash to finance the resulting lag and balance the running needs and resources.

It is the need in working capital, or more commonly called "working capital"

The following graph is visualizing the need in working capital through the typical cash balance structure of a production process.

Document 5 - PRODUCTION CASH BALANCE

NEEDS	RESOURCES
STOCKS	DOWNPAYMENTS RECEIVED
DOWNPAYMENTS MADE	TAX DEBTS
	DEBTS TO SUPPLIERS
RECEIVABLES FROM CLIENTS	NEED IN WORKING CAPITAL

Note : Unlike a Production business, a Services business may generate a (positive) resource in working capital : for instance a supermarket doesn't have any storage but its shelves, is paid upon delivery ("cash") by its Clients and usually pays its suppliers 60 or 90 days after receiving their invoices.

Such a "distribution" business is then a financial business, which growth is resulting from the financial performance of its positive cash balance.

1.5.2 Financing of the working capital

The Production cycle is made of 3 phases :

→ The 1st phase is the start-up of the activity :

An initial working capital shall be made available, that will allow to initiate labor payroll and handle the 1st lag between receivables and payables.
This initial working capital may be financed on equities or by a short term loan.
Like the interests during the investment period (see above), this burden may be added to the base load investment.

→ The 2nd phase is the production period, during which the actual need in working capital will fluctuate (market, prices, costs…) and may temporarily either exceed the initial working capital, or fall short.

The 1st situation will result in a shortfall of cash, while the 2nd situation will result in an excess.
A right management of the production process will lead to permanently balance needs and resources.

→ The 3rd phase is the end of the production cycle, or the end of the "monitoring period" of the financial study, after which the working capital is of no use any longer, and will be recovered as pure positive cash-flow.

1.6 Taxes

Tax implication shall be a case-by-case study, depending on the investor profile and the country where he may be liable to pay taxes.

Taxes, when applicable, have oftentimes a decisive impact on an investment opportunity.

1.6.1 VAT

VAT (value added tax) is generally not taken into account in a profitability analysis, as it is only subject to a tax *collection process*, therefore not impacting investor's cash-flows calculations.

1.6.2 Income tax

It is generally proportional to the gross income (though progressive for individuals in certain countries), and may be subject to certain exemptions or "grace periods", during which no income tax is due.

In case of financial losses during the production period or during the financial monitoring period, it may be possible to carry over the losses over the next profitable period, by means of tax deductions during a certain number of years.

1.6.3 Other taxes and incentives

The investment may be subject to materials import taxes and duties, services taxes, property taxes, regional taxes, taxes on capital gains, carbon taxes etc…

At the contrary, the investment may benefit certain incentives, when related to local manpower employment, environment protection and "green" energies.

These taxes and incentives will participate the cash-flows calculations and may impact the outcome of the profitability study.

1.7 Inflation

A profitability study can be made in current currency, or in constant currency of a given year.

1.7.1 Analysis in current currency

If CFa is the resulting cash flow of the year "a", its components (cfa1, cfa2....) shall be corrected by their own yearly price index "j", with year "1" as the reference year.

CFa = cfa1*(1 + j1)(a-1) + cfa2*(1 + j2)**(a-1)**

Note : In most of the cases, the specific price index of the different cash-flow components will remain un-known and will all be assumed to be equal to the general inflation "i".

Therefore :

CFa = cfa1*(1 + i)(a-1) + cfa2*(1 + i)**(a-1) + ...**

1.7.2 Analysis in constant currency

In constant currency of the year "n", the above cash-flow of the year "a" will be corrected (and therefore decreased) by the general inflation having depreciated the currency between the year "n" and the year "a".

Therefore above **CFa** will be divided by **(1 + i)**(a-n)**

Note : It is assumed that the yearly inflation remains the same in the period from year "n" to year "a".

If it is not the case, the above term shall be replaced by multiplying all terms (1 + ik) to each other, "ik" being the inflation at year "k", k varying from (n+1) to a.

Financial studies shall generally consider profitability criteria in both current and constant currency, in order to appreciate the effect of the inflation.

This effect may appear beneficial to the investor, for instance when revenues are inflated over the time, while loans repayments remain constant.

General note on symbols used in this guide :

"*" means "multiply by" (for instance 3 * 2 = 6)
"**" means "power" (for instance 3 ** 2 = 9)

CHAPTER 2

TIME VALUE AND DISCOUNTING

2.1 Psychological approach 18

2.2 Socio-political approach 19

2.3 Financial approach 19

2.4 Definition 19

2.5 Example 20

2.6 "Rationale" of discounting method 21

2.7 The value of the discount rate 23
    2.7.1 For a Corporation 23
    2.7.2 For States 24
    2.7.3 For individuals 25

CHAPTER 2

TIME VALUE AND DISCOUNTING

Common profitability criteria such as "ROI" (Return On Investment) or "Pay-out Time" have the merit to provide a simple evaluation of an investment, by offering a direct measure of the costs versus the gains, or of the time from which the gains are balancing the costs.

They can provide a quick answer to the question : "Is this investment profitable ?", but they can't however take into account the profile of the investment and resulting cash-flows along the years, and they can't always provide a sound analysis of the comparison between 2 investments options.

For instance, "Option 1" may have a larger ROI than "Option 2", but it will be also necessary to compare them under the angles of :

- Investment life cycle duration,
- Relative importance of up-front cash-flows versus late cash-flows
- Relative importance of the cash-flows after the Pay-out time has been reached
- Residual value of the investment at the end of the life cycle
- Ratio Equity/Loan
- Risk related to un-certain future

Another limitation of those "simple" criteria is that they don't implicitly take into account the option of "Doing nothing", for instance leaving the cash resources on the bank account at a certain yield.

Therefore, it is necessary to introduce the concepts of Time Value and Time discounting of the cash-flows, in the calculation of the main profitability criteria.

The concept of cash-flow discounting appeared in the years 1930', after the 1929 great depression. Investors became then careful when counting on future revenues without "weighing" them according to time and risk.

Actual implementation of the concept in usual analysis occurred later on with the emergence of computers, as it involves non-linear equations and calculations.

2.1 Psychological approach

It is a fact that 1 $ right now is always preferable to 1 $ next year.

This is due to the human nature to get needs satisfied immediately, to the limitation of human life span, to the future's uncertainty…

This means that 1 $ today is worth (1 + a) $ next year, where "a", thereafter named "discount rate", has a meaning of a quantified preference for the Present.

The present ("discounted") value of 1$ generated next year is then 1$/(1 + a).

This fact stands with or without inflation.

We are then ready to bear some "premium interest" for the immediate availability of an amount of money that can allow us to acquire goods or services now, instead of having to wait for it.

Another component of the meaning of the discount rate is the risk related to the uncertainty of the future remuneration of the investment.

There will generally be a discount rate without risk and and a rate covering the uncertainty risk, deriving from the first by adding a specific premium.

This aspect will be reviewed in Chapter 5.

We will consider situations in a "certain future" in chapters 2, 3 and 4, while risk appreciation will be discussed in chapter 5.

2.2 Socio-political approach

A high discount rate is reflecting a high propensity to spend immediately.

However, from the investor standpoint, this trend may be balanced by the high profitability of the potential projects he will then pre-select.

The resulting renouncement to spend (but to invest) is initiating growth.

The discount rate is then a peculiarity of a given economy or society, the ascertainment of its propensity to consume, or invest.

Authorities and Public regulators have means to orientate trends through discount rate, tax and other regulations.

2.3 Financial approach

The discount rate is a tool for arbitration between the present and the future, and allows to orientate investments choices.

For instance, if 2 technologies able to lead to the same production of the same product :

The first one requires a high investment but low subsequent expenses, and the second one is cheaper in investment but more expensive in operation costs.

The selection cannot be made only through the algebraic cumulating of their respective cash-flows.

That would – wrongly – imply that an immediate expense is equivalent to a future expense, and we know, or sense, that it is wrong.

Therefore, cash-flows must be "discounted" along the life cycle of the investment.

2.4 Definition

The present value of a future cash-flow CFn of year "n" is equal to :

CFn / (1 + a)**n, "a" being the discount rate.

This means that the future cash-flow of year "n" derives from its present value through its fictive investment at the interest rate "a" for n years.

Similarly, the Sum of the discounted cash-flows of an investment observed over a life cycle of n years, is :

$$S = \sum_{t=0}^{n} CFt / (1 + a)^{**}t$$

Or, if the Investment "I" is done at year "0" :

$$S = -I + \sum_{t=1}^{n} CFt / (1 + a)^{**}t$$

Such discounting of the cash-flows allows a comparison of investments options on the basis of the time distribution of their respective cash-flows.

2.5 Example

The Projects A and B with following investment profiles are to be compared :

Document 6 – NECESSITY OF DISCOUNTING CASH-FLOW

PROJECT A		PROJECT B	
Investment	1000	Investment	1000
Cash-Flow Year 1	100	Cash-Flow Year 1	400
Cash-Flow Year 2	300	Cash-Flow Year 2	400
Cash-Flow Year 3	500	Cash-Flow Year 3	400
Cash-Flow Year 4	700	Cash-Flow Year 4	400
Sum of Cash-Flows	1600	Sum of Cash-Flows	1600
Discounted Sum at 10%	193	Discounted Sum at 10%	268

The 2 investment projects have the same cumulated cash-flow over the 4 years observation period, but the Investment B has a much larger discounted cumulated cash-flow, at a 10% discount rate.

This allows to conclude that the Investment B has a better profitability in the sense of a better "quality", as more revenues are cashed-in in the early years of the observation period.

The "simple" pay-out time calculation would lead to the same conclusion, but it happens that discounting cash-flows is still necessary to arbitrate between 2 Investment projects having the same "simple" cumulated cash-flows and the same "simple" pay-out time.

For instance on longer economic observation periods, pay-out time criteria will remain blind on what is the cash-flow profile after pay-out time is reached, and what will be the (positive) residual value of the assets at the end of the period…

General note on symbols used in this guide :

"*" means "multiply by" (for instance 3 * 2 = 6)
"**" means "power" (for instance 3 ** 2 = 9)

2.6 "Rationale" of discounting method

Another approach highlights the rationale of discounting to appreciate an investment opportunity in a given economic environment.

"I" being an amount available at Year 0, there are 2 options for its owner to invest it from Year 0 to Year "n" :

1/ To invest it on the capital market (for instance in a bond) at the rate "a".

The future value at year "n" will be then : **I * (1 + a)**n**

2/ To invest it in a project and invest the resulting yearly cash-flows on the same capital market

The cumulated cash-flows "S" will be then :

$$S = \sum_{t=1}^{n} CF_t * (1 + a)^{**}(n - t)$$

(The cash-flow invested at Year "t" will indeed have a yearly return of "a" between Year "t" and Year "n").

The choice of investing "I" in the Project (rather than investing "I" on the bond market) shall only be made if the total return at Year "n" is bigger for the Project than for the bond market.

In other terms :

$$\sum_{t=1}^{n} CF_t * (1 + a)^{**}(n - t) > I * (1 + a)^{**}n$$

Which is equivalent to :

$$\sum_{t=1}^{n} CF_t * (1 + a)^{**}n / (1 + a)^{**}t > I * (1 + a)^{**}n$$

Or to :

$$- I + \sum_{t=1}^{n} CF_t / (1 + a)^{**}t > 0$$

In other words, to invest "I" in the Project will only make sense if the subsequent cumulated cash-flows discounted at the rate "a" is positive.

If it is equal to zero, it will be equivalent to invest "I" on the bond market or on the Project.

Note : We are assuming acting in a perfect world, where the risk of investing "I" in a Project is not more risky than to invest it on a reliable bond market, which is actually not quite right.

We will see in the next Chapter that the above formulae is nothing else than the Net Present Value ("NPV"), one of the most important profitability criteria used in economic and financial analysis.

2.7 The value of the discount rate

2.7.1 For a Corporation

The discount rate is depending upon the situation of the Investor :

a/ If the Investor is investing on equities, the discount rate will be determined as being its average actual profitability over the 5-10 last years.

For instance, if the past history of the Investor is showing an average profitability of 10% of the investments made along that period, then the Investor will select this rate as its discount rate, which is equivalent to select future Investments having an internal rate of return exceeding 10%.

We will see in the next Chapter another expression of the above statement :

The value of the Internal Rate of Return ("IRR") shall exceed the value of the discount rate, for the "NPV" to be positive, therefore for the Investment to be judged profitable.

b/ If the Investor is borrowing on the capital market, the discount rate will be determined as an average interest rate computed from the various sources of available capital, to which some risk margin will be added.

It will then represent the minimum discount rate to be used in further analysis, as it will lead to an "IRR", which shall be larger than the loan rate.

If the Investor is liable for income tax at the rate "T", then the minimum discount rate will be $b * (1 - T)$, b being the loan rate.

The Investor is then "saving" part of the loan interest through the applicable tax deduction.

The investor may also purposely increase the above discount rate, in order to select investments of higher profitability, and thus optimize the utilization of available capital.

2.7.2 For States

In the case of a planned economy or a State Enterprise, the choice of the discount rate is deriving from political orientations, and will constitute an important factor for a sustainable economic development.

The governments may elect to lower discount rates (thus to lower filtering) to encourage long term initiatives (for instance infrastructures designed to last 50 years or more....) that would benefit to next generations or boost the emergence of new technologies or green energies...

Too high discount rates would favor an immediate future and discourage to invest on a long term.

For instance when new technologies development starts, risk is high, return on investment is low, pay-out time long, and too high discount rates would kill such initiatives by implicit selection of less risky and more conventional options.

As an example, the discount rate used by the Public Planning in France is generally 4%, with a floor value of 2% for very long term initiatives.

Besides, this country is evaluating public investments initiatives on the basis of "certain cash-flows", by opposition to add a risk premium to the base discount rate.

"Certain cash-flows" means that the value of their components have been adjusted by statistical methods to set them at a maximum probability.

Last, the public evaluations are generally made in constant currency.

2.7.3 For individuals

For investment decisions at individual level, it is reasonable to choose a discount rate as reflecting an average return on a safe capital market (for instance bank deposit return or guaranteed bonds rate).

To be practical, taking a value within the range 1% to 3% is a reasonable approach (1% being the usual return of current bank account deposits and 3% being a fair bond return before tax).

CHAPTER 3

PROFITABILITY CRITERIA

3.1 Simple criteria 29
   3.1.1 Return On Investment (ROI) 29
   3.1.2 Pay-out Time 30

3.2 The main profitability criteria based on discounted cash-flows 31
   3.2.1 Net Present Value (NPV) 31
   3.2.2 Internal rate of return (IRR) 33
   3.2.3 Rate of Return on Equity (RRE) 34
   3.2.4 Pay-out time (or Pay-back time) 35
   3.2.5 Benefit / Cost Ratio (BCR) 35

3.3 Complementarity of the criteria and analysis 38
   3.3.1 NPV and IRR 38
   3.3.2 NPV and RRE 40
   3.3.3 NPV and Pay-out time 40

CHAPTER 3

PROFITABILITY CRITERIA

3.1 Simple criteria

As it has been mentioned in the previous chapter, there is a set of "simple" or "arithmetic" criteria able to provide an quick answer to the questions :

- Is this investment providing more earnings than expenses ?
- Do we make this investment or not ?
- How long will it take to get back my investment ?

3.1.1 Return On Investment (ROI)

The simple ROI is the measurement of the ratio Net Earnings / Investment Cost.

It is a common criterion providing an immediate picture of the profitability of a simple investment on a short period, but un-able to provide its user with an assessment of the investment risk and the earnings profile along the time.

Example : An investment of 100 will result in net earnings of 30 on Year 1, 40 on Year 2, 50 on Year 3 and 60 on Year 4, ie in total net earnings of 180.

The simple ROI will be then 180 / 100 = 1.8 = 180 %.

This ROI is then reflecting a fair profitability of the investment, but ignores what happens after the 4 years of economic observation, ignores how long it takes to the investor to get paid back.

Such standard ROI would be the same for an identical investment expenditure of 100 resulting in the same total net earnings of 180, but with 10 only on Year 1, 30 on Year 2, 50 on Year 3 and 90 on Year 4.

The 2 above investment options cannot obviously be compared through the sole use of the simple ROI, despite the identical investment cost.

Note : For investments resulting in yearly regular income, the Annual ROI is also commonly used, as the ratio Yearly Net Earnings / Investment Cost.

For instance, an investment of 100 resulting in a yearly net income of 45 will have an annual ROI of 45/100 = 45%.

3.1.2 Pay-out Time

The Pay-out time (or Pay-back time) is the arithmetic calculation of the time after which the cumulated net earnings are balancing the investment cost.

Example : For the 2 above investments options, the respective pay-out times are 2 year 7 months, and 3 years 1 month.

The value of this criterion is complementing the simple ROI calculations, but still ignores the time value of the cash-flows and what happens after the 4 years of the economic observation period.

Therefore, a sound profitability analysis shall use the below criteria and methodologies.

3.2 The main profitability criteria based on discounted cash-flows

3.2.1 Net Present Value (NPV)

It is the Sum of discounted cash-flows, cumulated from Year "0" to Year "n":

$$NPV = \sum_{t=0}^{n} CF_t / (1 + a)^{**t}$$

In the case of an investment disbursed at Year "0" (cash-flow = - I):

$$NPV = -I + \sum_{t=1}^{n} CF_t / (1 + a)^{**t}$$

In the case of an investment disbursed over the 2 first years:

$$NPV = -I_o - I_1 / (1 + a) + \sum_{t=2}^{n} CF_t / (1 + a)^{**t}$$

As per this criteria, the Investment will be judged "profitable" if:

NPV > 0.

Note: If NPV = 0, it is the break-even point, at which it is equivalent to invest or do nothing.

Following the same logic, In the case of 2 Investment options (IO 1 and IO 2) to be compared to each other, the Option IO 1 will be preferred to IO 2 if:

NPV 1 > NPV 2

This criteria is an hyperbolic function of the discount rate.

From the below graph representing this function, the value of the discount rate for which the NPV = 0 is by definition the "Internal Rate of Return" (IRR), without any external financing contribution.

Document 7 – NPV versus DISCOUNT RATE

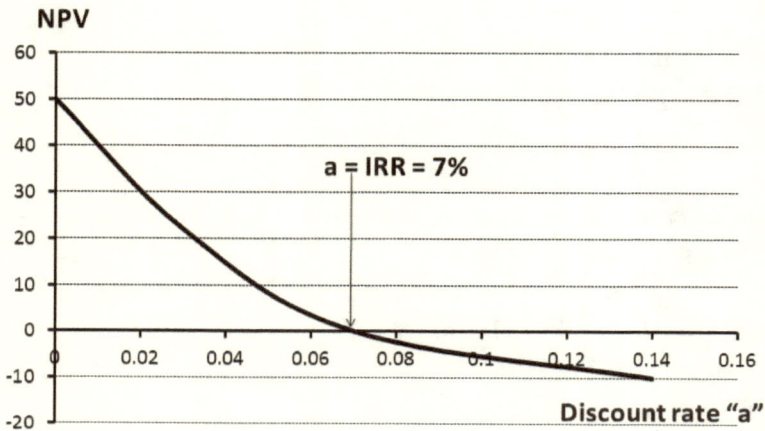

In the case of identical cash-flows over the investment observation period :

$$NPV = -I + CF * \sum_{t=1}^{n} 1 / (1 + a)^{**}t$$

with : $\sum_{t=1}^{n} 1 / (1 + a)^{**}t = [1 - (1 + a)^{**}(-n)] / a$

General note on symbols used in this guide :

"*" means "multiply by" (for instance 3 * 2 = 6)
"**" means "power" (for instance 3 ** 2 = 9)

3.2.2 Internal rate of return (IRR)

The very definition of this criterion is displayed on above graph.
The IRR is the discount rate for which the NPV is equal to 0.
It quantifies the inherent profitability of an investment on investor's equity, without the contribution of external financing.

→ The IRR of an investment must be larger than the investor's discount rate, in order to qualify this investment as "profitable".
→ **If IRR = a, then NPV = 0** and *to invest* or *to not invest* are equivalent decisions, if we ignore at this stage any consideration due to risk.
→ **If IRR < a, then VNA < 0** and the investment subject to the analysis must be abandoned.

Following the same logic, In the case of 2 Investment options (I O1 and I O2) to be compared to each other, the Option I O1 will be preferred to IO 2 if :

IRR 1 > IRR 2

Note : Computers applications or usual spreadsheets are providing formulas for IRR calculations from Investment, yearly cash-flows and discount rate values.

Practically, it may also be convenient for simple investment cases, to proceed by "trials and errors", ie approaching the discount rate for which NPV is 0.

The IRR shall not be mixed up with the "simple" ROI, which is, as introduced above, the ratio of the yearly average cash-flow to the initial investment.

However, their values can be close to each other, when :

- The yearly cash-flows are identical
- The observation period is short
- The investment residual value is negligible.

Last, beside his role of profitability criterion of an investment, the IRR is determining the maximal loan rate that would be necessary to finance the Investment, partly or totally.

In other words, if the investor were to borrow the whole amount of the investment at an interest rate equal to the IRR, the Sum of discounted cumulated cash-flows would be equal to 0 at the end of the observation period.

3.2.3 Rate of Return on Equity (RRE)

Its definition is similar to IRR's, in the case of an external financing.

The loan components (capital and yearly interests) are here taken into account in the cash-flows calculations and the NPV of the global initiative (Investment + Financing).

RRE is then the discount rate for which this "global NPV" is equal to 0.

Unlike the IRR (which quantifies the profitability of the whole investment on equities), the RRE will then quantify the profitability of the sole equity invested, the rest of the required capital being subject to a loan.

The IRR is then the indication of the inherent profitability of a "stand-alone" investment, while the RRE is the actual measurement of the global investment operation, including the external financing.

Several investment options will then be compared on the basis of their respective IRRs (and NPVs), but once an option has been selected, it has to be validated through the calculation of the RRE, which takes into account the financing scheme.

Note : In the reality, capital availability is limited and the required external financing is the most critical hurdle to overcome, whatever the potential profit it could lead to.

We will study on next chapters how IRR turns into a larger RRE through the "leverage effect", when the loan rate meets certain conditions.

3.2.4 Pay-out time (or Pay-back time)

It is probably the most commonly used criteria, but as a paradox, also the most limited in its ability to provide a comprehensive view of an investment's profitability.

This is certainly due to our impatience and appetite for the present, and to our natural concern on risks carried by a far future.

The Pay-out time is defined as the time from which the discounted cumulated cash-flow becomes positive.

In other terms, it is the time required for the earnings to balance the initial investment.

It shall derive from discounted cash-flows calculations.

However generally, investors are meaning it in terms of non-discounted cash-flows, partly due to a lack of induction to these concepts.

It is to note that discounting of cash-flows leads to increase the pay-out time.

However, as selected investment are generally supposed to have a short pay-out time, the effect of discounting, ie dividing by $(1 + a)^{**}t$, is not significantly impacting the Pay-out time over the first few years.

In any case, it shall be précised if the pay-out time relates or not to discounted cash-flows, in order to avoid misunderstandings.

Last, a Pay-out time is always related to the Equity injected in the investment, whatever the ratio Equity/Loan.

3.2.5 Benefit / Cost Ratio (BCR)

It is the discounted net cumulated revenues divided by the initial investment. It must be higher than 1.

It is sometimes used for public investments to rank Projects among each others. However, it shall not be used alone as a criterion of selection, as it may outrank projects with lower BCR, but having larger NPV.

The following schematic is summarizing how the main profitability criteria participate the analysis of an industrial investment.

Simple individual investments or financial operations are studied on the same logic.

Currency depreciation may not be always considered when short periods are considered.

Document 8 - FRAME OF A CORPORATE INVESTMENT ANALYSIS

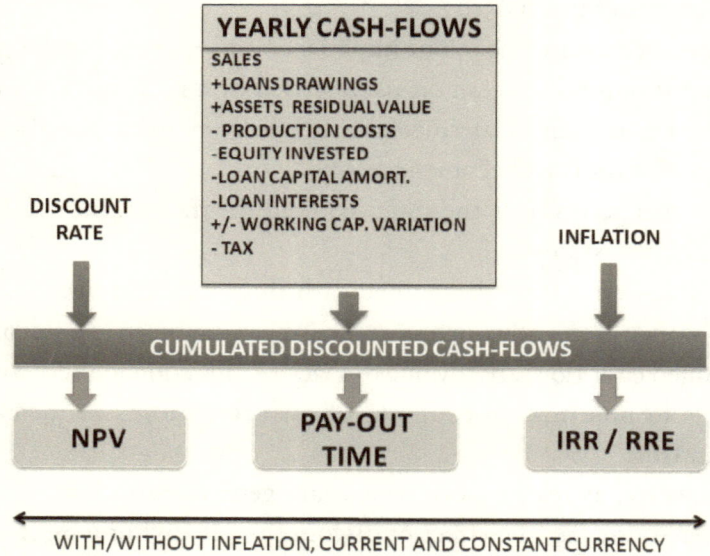

The next schematic visualizes what the investment cash-flow table is revealing in terms of profitability analysis :

Document 9 - MAIN PROFITABILITY CRITERIA

ECONOMIC OBSERVATION PERIOD

YEAR	1	2	3	-------	k	---------	n
DISCOUNTED CASH-FLOW	CF1 < 0	CF2 < 0	CF3 > 0	-------	CFk > 0	---------	CFn > 0
CUMULATED DISCOUNTED CASH-FLOW	CF1 < 0	Sum CF 1->2 < 0	Sum CF 1->3 < 0	-------	Sum CF 1->k = 0	---------	Sum CF 1->n > 0

INVESTMENT PERIOD — PAY-OUT TIME — NPV

CONSTRUCTION CAPEX PERIOD — PRODUCTION OPEX PERIOD

Note : Study cases calculation spreadsheets are provided on our companion website at :

https://www.investments-profitability-calculations-ericmatter.com

3.3 Complementarity of the criteria and analysis

A decision to invest, or a selection among different investment options, shall not rely on a single criteria, but shall be based on a global analysis of all of them, as they have complementary meanings.

3.3.1 NPV and IRR

The below document is displaying the graphs "NPV versus IRR" for 2 investments options :

Option 1 is defined by NPV 1 and IRR 1
Option 2 is defined by NPV 2 and IRR 2

NPV 1 and NPV 2 are the respective Net Present Values of the two Projects, and are defined at the same discount rate, as the Investor is the same.

Document 10 – ANALYSIS NPV versus IRR

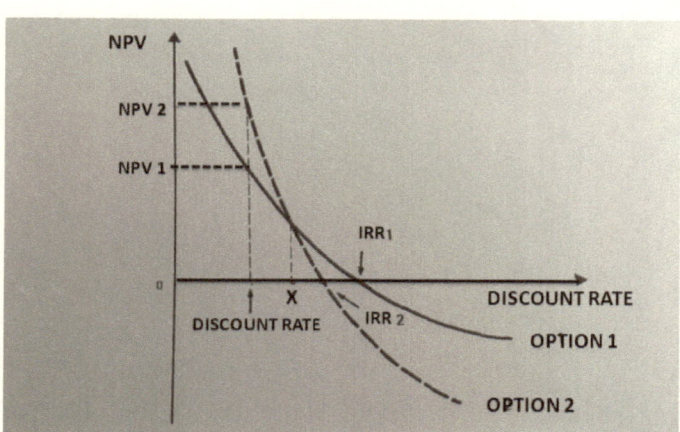

We can see that if IRR was the only criterion to analyse, Option 1 would be retained, while by focusing on NPV only, Option 2 would be selected.

The value "x" obtained at the crossing of the 2 graphs is the discount rate for which NPV 1 = NPV 2.

- NPV is an "additive" quantity expressed in monetary unit, tangible and immediately perceptible. The reliability of its value is however depending on an accurate knowledge of the investor's discount rate, which is not always obvious.
- IRR is less concrete and results from other criteria (discounting cash-flows and then extracting the rate at which NPV = 0), but remains however familiar to those handling financial studies or evaluating investments. IRR shall mainly remain a basis for a decision "invest – don't invest", by comparison to the usual discount rate of the investor. Its utilization in the comparison of 2 investment options shall be cautiously handled : the respective IRRs of 2 investment options are indeed nothing else than "fictive" (or "equivalent") discount rates for which their respective NPVs become zero. IRR shall instead be used to select an external financing, which leverage effect will be positive if its rate is smaller than the IRR.

So to conclude on the analysis displayed on above graph, a recommended approach will be :

- To select the investment option having the largest NPV value (here NPV 2)
- Check that the IRR of the selected option (here IRR 2) still remains larger than the maximum rate of a possible external loan, even though IRR 2 is here smaller than IRR 1.
- Determine the effect of the external financing (leverage effect) by calculating the RRE (Return of investment on equity) and the global NPV (including the financing – related cash-flows)
- Continue the investigation with other criteria.

3.3.2 NPV and RRE

Once the parameters of the financing loan will be known (debt/equity ratio, nature of the loan, rate, duration, repayment mode…), they shall be integrated into the global profile of the selected option, in order to determine the global NPV and the RRE.

The global NPV is the discounted cumulated cash-flow related to the investment combined with the loan. The RRE is equivalent to the IRR, but related to the own funds (equities) of the investor. It is also by definition the discount rate at which the global NPV is zero.

In the previous comparison between the 2 options, it is advised to also double-check the global NPV and the RRE of the option that has been discarded (here option 1).

The option that will ultimately carry the largest global NPV will be definitely selected.

3.3.3 NPV and Pay-out time

The selection study of the previous study case is not over yet. The option 2 is has been selected on the basis of a larger NPV. The below graph displays the evolution of the cumulated cash-flow of the 2 options along time.

Document 11 – ANALYSIS NPV versus Pay-out Time

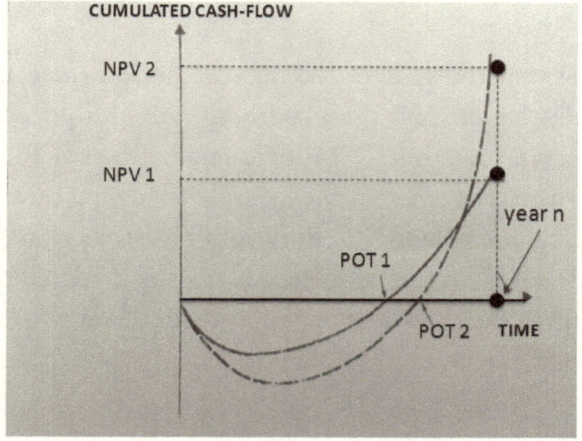

At the year "n", end of the period of economic observation, the final values of the respective cumulated cash-flows are par definition the NPVs of the 2 options.

This analysis is bringing another important information linked to the capitalistic value of an investment : Although the Option 2 has been selected for its higher profitability, its investment value is higher and its pay-out time is longer.

NPV and and Pay-out time are then leading to contradictory conclusions and the final decision will be made on more subjective criteria, depending on the investor profile and his attitude in front of the risk carried by an un-certain future :

- If the investor prefers to engage a higher capital to gain higher profits, and can accept to get it paid back later, he will select the Option 2.
- If he prefers instead to limits his financial commitment, get it paid back sooner and can accept a lower profitability, he will then select the Option 1.
- If his resources and access to financing are limited, he will have to comply with the constraint and to go for Option 1.

Though the pay-out time is only providing a limited view of the profitability of an investment option, it appears to be widely considered as a major criteria by investors. This conservative attitude is reflecting an important concern for the risk linked to an un-certain future. It may lead to economic non-senses, as an investment is essentially meant to create sustainable growth and wealth, more than to be necessarily paid-back soonest.

Conclusions :

a. If it is about studying the profitability of a single investment opportunity, it shall be checked that :

- NPV > 0

- IRR > Discount rate
- Loan rate < IRR (excluding tax deduction)

The financing leverage effect will be then obtained by measuring the gap between RRE and IRR. Last, the value of the Pay-out time will be compared to the usual acceptable range for that investment.

b. If it is about comparing several investment options for the selection of one of them, the highest NPV shall be the first decisive criterion and the resulting IRR will allow to check that an external financing, if available, can be applied and improve the economics.

Then the options ranked as per above criteria will be screened under the angle of the capital to mobilize, and the length of the pay-out time, to appreciate the risk they are carrying.

Note : If it is recommended to use the NPV as the primary criteria, we remind that it requires a sound appreciation of the investor discount rate, which may not be obvious. The IRR instead is a less intuitive concept, but the calculation of its value does not require the knowledge of the discount rate.

Chapter 4

Influence of External Financing and Inflation

4.1 Leverage effect of external financing 45
    4.1.1 Global approach 45
    4.1.2 Analytical approach 46

4.2 Effect of inflation 49

CHAPTER 4

Influence of External Financing and Inflation

4.1 Leverage effect of external financing

Industrial investments will require external financing, typically within a range 50% - 80% of the capital to invest.

For smaller or individual initiatives, the investor may or may not borrow on the financial markets.

4.1.1 Global approach

As outlined earlier, IRR is not only a indicator of the intrinsic profitability of an investment, but also the indication of the maximum rate value of the loan that will finance it.

In order to take into account the tax applied on profits, it is reminded that the Loan IRR, or net actuarial rate, is : $IRR = j*(1 - i)$, with :

j being the loan rate
i being the tax rate

The inclusion of a loan into an investment scheme will lead to the obtention of a "global NPV", by taking into account the cash-flows related to the loan draw and to the repayment of the capital and interests. As described earlier, it will then lead to the RRE (Rate of Return on Equities), which is the discount rate at which that global NPV is zero.

The difference between IRR and RRE will then measure the leverage effect brought by the loan, which can be positive or negative. Once the external financing profile is known, the global NPV and the RRE will constitute the main indicators of the profitability for the global initiative (investment + related financing), together with the pay-out time.

The investor can face 2 different situations :

a/ The loan is a must (large investments) and its profile (Loan IRR, duration, amount) is imposed by the lender..

→ If loan IRR > Investment IRR, the resulting global NPV will be then lower than the investment NPV, and the RRE will be lower than the IRR. The application of the external financing is downgrading the profitability of the investment, but it does not necessarily mean that the global initiative must be abandoned.

If the global NPV still remains positive, and if RRE is till higher than the investor's discount rate, the initiative may be pursued.

→ If loan IRR < Investment IRR, RRE will be higher than IRR, and the global NPV may be lower or higher than the investment NPV. The global profitability is then enhanced by the external financing, which acts as a positive leverage.

b/ The investor is not obliged to contract a loan and can decide the amount to borrow.

→ If loan IRR > Investment IRR, the investor will check that the resulting global NPV still remains at an acceptable (positive) level. If the initiative is not risky and if there is no alternative investment possibility, it will be preferable to *not* finance the investment with a loan.
→ If loan IRR < Investment IRR, RRE will be higher than IRR and the investor will preferentially contract a loan, which amount will depend on the leverage induced on the NPV

4.1.2 Analytical approach

As an investment NPV is a decreasing function of the discount rate, the loan NPV is an increasing function of the discount rate. The intersection of the loan NPV with the discount rate axis is the loan IRR, as defined above.

This approach is then consisting in separating the investment (on equities) study from the loan study, and use the "additive" properties of the NPV criterion, to decide their merging into a global initiative.

Note : The investment initiative has an initial cash-out and subsequent cash-in milestones, while the loan initiative has an initial cash-in (loan draw) and subsequent cash-out milestones. This similarity allows an identical analysis of the two initiatives.

The first graph below is displaying the variations of investment NPV and loan NPV versus discount rate, in the case : loan IRR < investment IRR.

The resulting global NPV is the algebraic sum of the investment NPV and the loan NPV, and this global NPV may be lower or higher than the NPV of the Investment alone, depending on the value of the investor's discount rate.

In the below graph, the global NPV is slightly lower than the investment NPV, but still at a relatively high value, that would keep the initiative viable. This is describing a typical situation where a loan is necessary, and where the investor has to check its effect on the profitability.

**Document 12 – ANALYSIS Investment versus loan
Case IRR Loan < IRR Investment**

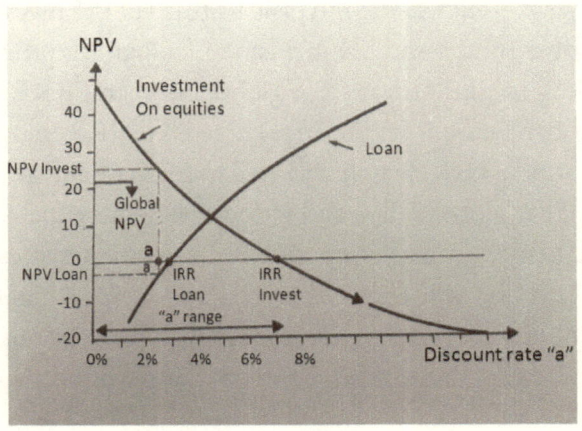

The second below graph describes the case Loan IRR > Investment IRR, where the resulting global NPV will be lower than the investment IRR alone.

There is then no point to contract a loan, unless the investor is short of funds.

**Document 13 – ANALYSIS Investment versus loan
Case IRR Loan > IRR Investment**

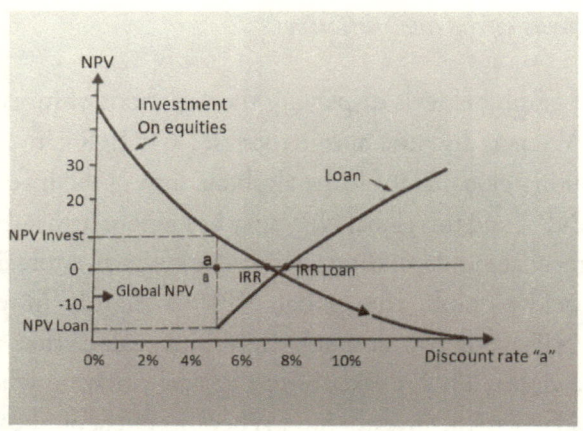

Conclusions :

- NPV and IRR are the intrinsic features of the investment alone (on own funds) and the inclusion of a loan into the initiative is leading to similar features : global NPV and RRE.
- The loan amount will be maximized if its IRR is lower than the investment IRR, which will lead to higher RRE and eventually to higher global NPV, and to lower Pay-out time.
- If a loan is mandatory and if its characteristics are fixed, the investor will check that RRE is *at least* higher than his discount rate, and that the global NPV is *at least* positive, before proceeding. The resulting pay-out time will be also analyzed.

- If 2 investment initiatives have already been compared on own funds, the resulting selection shall be checked after the inclusion of a loan.

4.2 Effect of inflation

Discounting of cash-flows in constant currency is conservative. However it doesn't allow the investor to appreciate the (sometimes) positive effects of the relative inflation of the components of these cash-flows.

As introduced earlier :

→ In current currency, if CFa is the resulting cash flow of the year "a", its components (cfa1, cfa2….) shall be corrected by their own yearly price index "j", with year "1" as the reference year :

CFa = cfa1*(1 + j1)**(a-1) + cfa2*(1 + j2)**(a-1)

Note : In most of the cases, the specific price index of the different cash-flow components will remain un-known and will all be assumed to be equal to the general inflation "i". Therefore :

CFa = cfa1*(1 + i)**(a-1) + cfa2*(1 + i)**(a-1) + …

→ In constant currency of the year "n", the above cash-flow of the year "a" will be corrected (and therefore decreased) by the general inflation having depreciated the currency between the year "n" and the year "a".

Therefore above **CFa** will be divided by **(1 + i)**(a-n)**

Note : It is assumed that the yearly inflation remains the same in the period from year "n" to year "a".

If it is not the case, the above term $(1 + i)^{**}(a - n)$ shall be replaced by multiplying all terms $(1 + ik)$ to each other, "ik" being the inflation at year "k", k varying from $(n+1)$ to a.

Financial studies shall generally consider profitability criteria in both current and constant currency, in order to appreciate the effect of the inflation.

This effect may appear beneficial to the investor, for instance when revenues are inflated over the time, while loans repayments remain constant.

Note : If the discounted cash-flows schedule is established in current currency, it is possible to neutralize the effect of inflation by increasing the discount rate with the inflation rate.

Demonstration :

If "a" is the discount rate,

If "i" is the general inflation rate,

If a' is the discount rate in current currency

$(1 + a') = (1 + a)*(1 + i) = 1 + a + i + a*i$

The term a*i being negligible as a and i have small values, we get :

$a' = a + i$

If "j" is the yearly increase index of the cash-flow in current currency, if CFo is its initial value, and if CF' is the cash-flow in current currency :

$CF't = CFo*(1 + j)^{**}t$

The corresponding discounted cash-flow CFA't, discounted with the rate a' is then :

$$CFA't = CFo*(1+j)**t / (1+a')**t = CFo*(1+j)**t / (1+a+i)**t, \text{ or}$$

$$CFA't = CFo*(1+j)**t / \{(1+a)**t * (1+i)**t\}$$

This method, though not mandatory, leads to obtain the same discounted cash-flows than those obtained in constant currency :

The previous cash-flow expressed in constant currency is :

$$CFt = CF't / (1+i)**t = CFo*(1+j)**t / (1+i)**t$$

The corresponding discounted cash-flow CFAt, discounted with the rate a is :

$$CFAt = CFo*(1+j)**t / \{(1+a)**t * (1+i)**t\}$$

Then, $CFAt = CFA't$

CHAPTER 5

RISK ANALYSIS AND EVALUATION IN UN-CERTAIN FUTURE

5.1 Integration of un-certainty to the analysis 58
    5.1.1 Practical example 58
    5.1.2 Main methods 59

5.2 Usual methodologies to help the decision 60
    5.2.1 Sensivity analysis 60
    5.2.2 Scenario analysis 61
    5.2.3 Basic probabilistic approach 62
    5.2.4 Decision table 65
    5.2.5 Decision tree 68
    5.2.6 Other methods 71

5.3 Monte-Carlo analysis 72
    5.3.1 Principles 72
    5.3.2 Random numbers generation 72
    5.3.3 Probability laws selection 73
    5.3.4 Inter-dependence between parameters 76
    5.3.5 Analysis of the simulation 77
    5.3.6 Influence of the random sampling size 80

5.4 Global approach and flexibility : Real Options 81

Chapter 5

Risk Analysis and Evaluation in Un-Certain Future

Above chapters introduced to profitability analysis in a "certain future", whereby the expected cash-flows of an investment plan are supposed to actually materialize.

However, as underlined in a book of one of the most famous economists (J.M. Keynes), the future is by nature subject to un-certainty, and so does a given economic environment that constitute the basis of a profitability study.

Such components of a discounted cash-flow, as profit, market, credit availability, tax policy, inflation, interests rates, discount rates, currency exchange… are subject to un-foreseeable variations along the period of the economic observation.

An investment decision grounded on the sole appreciation of the profitability criteria in a certain future, will put the investor at *risk* to miss his objectives or select the wrong option.

An investment is then carrying a potential *return* which goes along with a certain *risk* affecting its prevision, and a sound decision process shall then acknowledge and appreciate both side of the same coin : return and risk.

The risks affecting the various components of an investment may be first treated in 4 different ways, as summarized below : avoid, transfer, mitigate or accept.

Document 14 – Risk handling

THE IMPORTANCE OF A RISK IS DEFINED BY ITS PROBABILITY AND BY ITS IMPACT IF IT OCCURS.
4 ACTIONS CAN BE TAKEN ACCORDING ACORDING TO THE COUPLE PROBABILITY-IMPACT.

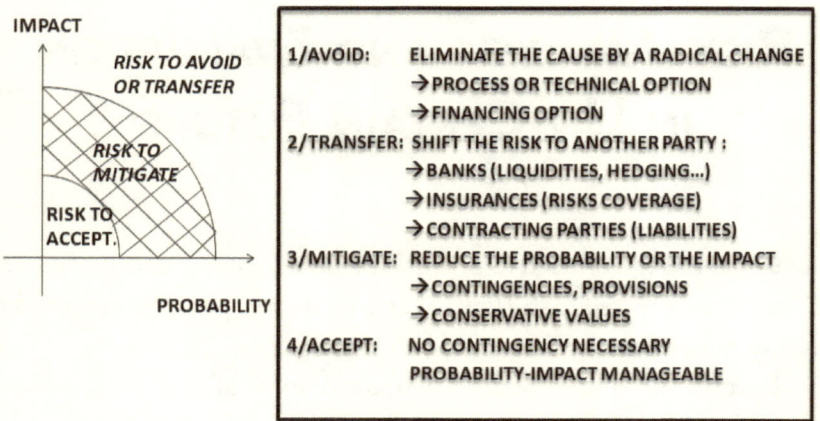

A discounted cash-flow will be composed of the following parameters, each of them affected by respective risks :

- Sales ← market risk, transformation process risk, currency exchange…
- Expenses ← raw materials availability risk, utilities cost risk, labor cost risk…
- Loan capital ← funds raising risk…
- Interest rate ← risk due to market fluctuations and government policies…
- Inflation rate ← risk due to domestic and international economic environment
- Tax rate ← risk due to government policy change…
- Discount rate ← risk due to the relevance of the value…

Each of these risks shall be then adequately treated during the pre-selection of investment options, prior to analyzing their potential profitability.

For instance :

- Market risk will be *mitigated* by prudent sales figures, volumes and prices
- Process risk will be *avoided* by the selection of a well-proven technology, even though less cost-effective,
- Currency exchange risk will be avoided through currency options contracts or *transferred* to insurance market through hedging,
- Raw material availability risk will be *transferred* to suppliers through subcontracts with constraining liabilities,
- Utilities tariff risk will be *mitigated* by long term tariffs or proper contingencies,
- Labor cost risk will be *mitigated* by long term policies and negotiation with unions,
- Funds raising risk will be partly *transferred* via proper guarantees and insurances,
- Interest rate risk will be *mitigated* through reasonable contingencies,
- Inflation rate risk will be *mitigated* by taking conservative values,
- Tax rate risk will be *accepted* as policies generally stand on long term,
- Discount rate un-certainty will be *accepted* and later on subject to sensitivity analysis…
- Export risk will be transferred to banks through export credits and political risks to specific insurance agencies such COFACE in France, SACE in Italy, SINOSURE in China…

Such a treatment will minimize the "residual risk" affecting the components of profitability criteria, and will maximize the quality and reliability of the results.

This residual risk, or un-certainty on some of these components, is the subject of the next chapters.

5.1 Integration of un-certainty to the analysis

5.1.1 Practical example

The following graph illustrates the obvious importance of risk and un-certainty in the evaluation of investment options profitability :

Assuming that an investor must select one option among the 3 following :

- Option A, having an expected NPV of 13 MM $ (highest probability)
- Option B, having an expected NPV of 23 MM $.
- Option C, having an expected NPV of 20 MM $.

Document 15 – Selection of an option according to probability distribution

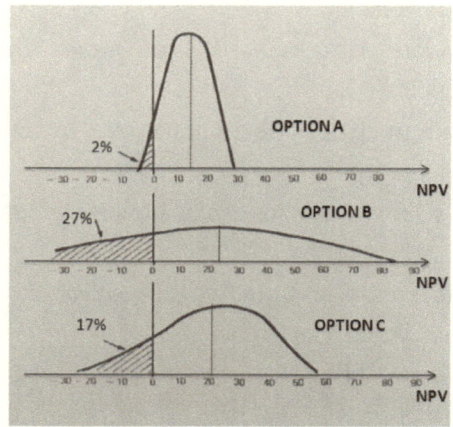

As per a standard analysis in a certain future, it would appear justified to select the option B, having the highest NPV.

However, the above graphs are providing additional information on the probability distribution of the NPV value for each option and their teaching may question such above selection :

- Option A, despite a relatively low NPV of 13 MM $, has only 2% chances of having an NPV lower than zero, and about the same probability to have an NPV > 25 MM $.
- Option B has the highest expected NPV (23 MM $), but its value may be negative with a probability of 27%. However, NPV may exceed 70 MM $.
- Option C is an an intermediate situation between options A and B.

Conclusions :

Although option B has the highest expected NPV, it is also the most risky, as significant chances are there to get a negative or low profitability.

It appears then more reasonable to select for instance the option C, safer than B, but still more risky than A.

That additional risk compared to A may be judged justified by a relatively high probability to get a higher profitability than the expected value.

This example is showing that a study in certain future is necessary but not sufficient to support a sound decision.

Last, the attitude of the investor in front of the risk, or the standard procedures of a corporation in a risky environment, will be decisive for a final selection.

5.1.2 Main methods

There are 2 main methods to integrate the un-certain nature of the future into the outcome of a profitability analysis :

A. To adjust the discount rate with an additional "risk premium" that is supposed to "cover" the global un-certainty affecting the profitability of the investment, based to cash-flows discounting.

That method is preferred by financial markets and is used by public investors.

Its weak point lies however on the evaluation of that risk premium, and on the fact that it does not always reflect the variation of the global risk of an investment option along the time.

In some situations, for instance a public investment in a bridge or in a highway, risks are tangible during the early phase (final CAPEX, captive market, start-up success, sales ramp-up…) and tend to decrease along the time, while to top-up the discount rate with such a premium will implicitly mean that the risk profile is uniform over the whole economic observation period.

B. To keep the actual discount rate of the investor but identify and quantify the most important un-certainties through probability assessment, and obtain the most probable resulting value of the profitability criteria, for instance the NPV.

This method is called "equivalent to certain", as it provides the most likely value of the profitability, according to the actual probability distribution of the parameters.

It is used for instance by France for public investments.

Next chapters are offering different methodologies to analyze or quantify un-certainties and probabilities.

5.2 Usual methodologies to help the decision

5.2.1 Sensivity analysis

A profitability analysis is using a simulation model (see our dedicated website www.investments-profitability-calculations-ericmatter.com) using formulas.

These formulas are composed of parameters subject to some degree of un-certainty.

It is then recommended, as a minimum evaluation of the risk, to study the sensitivity of the model to the variation of certain parameters, one at a time.

For instance, the variation of the NPV value will be recorded, according to the variation of such parameters as profit, taxation rate, inflation, interest rate etc..., one by one.

It will be then determined to which parameters the NPV calculation is the most sensitive, and from there what is the level of the risk taken by the investor, if these parameters are actually subject to wide un-certainty.

The obvious limit of such analysis is its "mono-variable" nature, not allowing a conclusive response to the variation of several parameters simultaneously.

As a practical example, in European Commission, when assessing investments, a critical parameter is defined as such when a variation of 1% of its value leads to a variation of 5% of NPV value.

5.2.2 Scenario analysis

Several parameters may be grouped as reflecting a specific macro-economic background, or global "scenario".

They may be then simultaneously changed to study the response of the model (for instance the NPV) to a change of the background.

For instance, the NPV response of an investment option may be analyzed in a high economic growth environment, and compared it to its value in an economically depressed environment.

A high economic growth environment will be for instance characterized by higher volumes of sales, higher raw materials and labor costs, higher inflation rate and lower interests rate, and possibly higher discount rate (acting as a more severe profitability filter, due to a higher number of investment options).

The NPV value may also be analyzed according to the international financial situation (credit availability or scarcity, high or low interest rates, foreign currencies exchange situation etc...), whereby several parameters will be adjusted simultaneously and in a consistent way.

5.2.3 Basic probabilistic approach

There are different approaches based on probability laws, to take into account the un-certainty affecting the parameters of profitability criteria :

- Estimate each parameter by its *mode*, i.e. define its most probable value.
  This is the "mode estimate".
- Estimate each parameter by its *mean*, i.e. the weighted average of all its possible values.
  This is the "average estimate" or "mean estimate".
- Take for each parameter the value that has a certain probability to be exceeded if it is a benefit, or the value that has a certain probability to be not exceeded if it is a cost.
  These probabilities are fixed *a priori* by the investor or analyst.
  This is the "minimal estimate", or "prudent estimate".

These approaches reflect different attitudes in front of the risk.

The first and second prioritize what seems to be the most likely to happen.

The third aims at avoiding an option that should not deserve to be selected, but also ignores by doing so, the risk of discarding options that would still deserve consideration.

However, the results obtained from these methods are not consistent with the attitudes they are supposed to derive from.

Example :

The following table provides the probability distribution with of a product selling price *versus* sold quantities.

	PRICE = 10	PRICE = 5
QUANTITY = 100	60 %	80%
QUANTITY = 50	40%	20%

On top of it, the price of the good varies according to following probabilities :

PRICE	10	5
PROBABILITY	60 %	40%

a/ Mode Estimate

The probability to sell 100 units is then :
60% * 60% + 40% * 80% = 68%

The probability to sell 50 units is then :
60% * 40% + 40% * 20% = 32%

The estimate by the *mode* leads then to take the price of 10 and the quantity of 100, therefore to estimate sales at **1000**.

However, according to above tables, the probability distribution of the sales is the following :

PRICE	QUANTITIES	SALES	PROBABILITY
10	100	1000	36%
10	50	500	24%
5	100	500	32%
5	50	250	8%

The most probable value of the sales is then **500**, with a probability of 24% + 32% = 56%

→ it is then contrary to the conclusions of an estimate by the *mode*, that was giving **1000**.
→ The mode estimate does not give then necessarily the most probable value.

b/ Average Estimate

Based on the same above set of data, the average price is then :
10 * 60% + 5 * 40% = 8

The average quantity is then :
100 * 68% + 50 * 32% = 84

The estimate by the *average* leads then to estimate sales at 8 * 84 = **672.** However, according to the same above table, the calculated average sales is :

1000 * 36% + 500 * 56% + 250 * 8% = **660**

→ The 2 results are different (though not far from each other), essentially because the 2 parameters are not independent from each other, which is oftentimes the case.
→ The consistency of the average estimate is then questionable as well.

c/ Prudent Estimate

Still on the basis of the above set of data, if we choose to retain for the most beneficial values, those having more than 60% probability to be exceeded, we will then take :

- 10 for the price (P = 60%)
- 100 for the quantity (P = 68% as calculated above)

The *prudent estimate* of the sales will be then 1000.

→ It is again different from the value provided by the above table, whereby the probability for the sales to exceed 1000 is only 36%.
→ Here again, there is un-consistency.

Conclusion :

The above basic approaches do not procure an efficient help to the decision.

Using a probabilistic approach will require to involve the distribution laws of probability of the parameters, as it will be presented in Chapter 5.3

5.2.4 Decision table

An investor has to select one of the following options in an un-certain environment which may be competitive, or not competitive :

- Invest
- Don't invest (keep cash resources on safe financial markets)

The summary of the total revenues resulting from each case, are :

	INVEST	DON'T INVEST
COMPETITION	- 100	+ 150
NO COMPETITION	+ 500	+ 150

The decision may be helped using different criteria reflecting different attitudes in front of the un-certainty :

a/ Laplace criteria

It is the average value of the revenues for both possible decisions :

- For "INVEST", the average revenue is + 200
- For "DON'T INVEST", the average revenue is + 150

The decision will be then "INVEST", as it leads to the higher average value.

b/ Minimax criteria

It is assumed that to select the option "INVEST" will mobilize all the resources of the investor. Therefore, if the choice does not reveal profitable, it would turn a financial disaster for the investor.

The criteria is then to minimize the maximum loss.

In the above situation, it will lead then to select the option "DON'T INVEST", which eliminates the risk of loosing 100 in a competitive environment.

This attitude will never lead an investor to "strike" on a tempting opportunity, but may preserve his resources on the long term.

c/ Maximax criteria

It is the highest expected revenue from all situations, and will lead here to select the option "INVEST", as the maximum expected revenue is 500 in a non-competitive environment.

d/ Maximin criteria

It is the highest of the minimum value in from all situations, and will lead here to select the option "DON'T INVEST", as the highest of the two minimum revenues in each option is 150.

This criterion is then about minimizing the risk.

e/ Regret minimization criteria

- Assuming the investor is selecting the option "DON'T INVEST", with an environment revealing non-competitive. The revenues will then amount +150. His question would be now : how much would have I earned if I would have selected the option "INVEST" ? The answer is : +500.

He would then "regret" to miss 500 − 150 = +350

- Assuming now that the investor is selecting the option "INVEST", with an environment revealing competitive. The revenues will then amount -100. His question would be now : how much would have I earned if I would have selected the option "DON'T INVEST" ? The answer is : +150

He would then "regret" to miss 150 − (-100) = +250

→ The maximum regret (of having selected the wrong option) is +350, corresponding to the selection of "DON'T INVEST".
→ As the criteria is to minimize the regret, the investor will then finally select the option "INVEST".

f/ Subjective weighing criteria

It is assumed that the probability for the environment to be competitive is 25% (and 75% for non-competitive).
By weighing the 2 situations by their respective probabilities, it is then possible to get a weighted value of the revenues for each option :

- INVEST : -100 * 25% + 500 * 75% = 350
- DON'T INVEST : 150 * 25% + 150 * 75% = 150

The application of this criteria will then lead to select the option "INVEST".

Conclusion :

Out of the 6 above criteria used to help a decision, 4 of them are leading to select the option "INVEST" and 2 of them are leading to the opposite choice.
This outcome does not necessarily conclude to finally select the option "INVEST", but reflects the actual difficulty to arbitrate between investment options in an un-certain environment.

5.2.5 Decision tree

The decision tree built on above example is displayed in following document.

Document 16 – Decision tree – 1st example

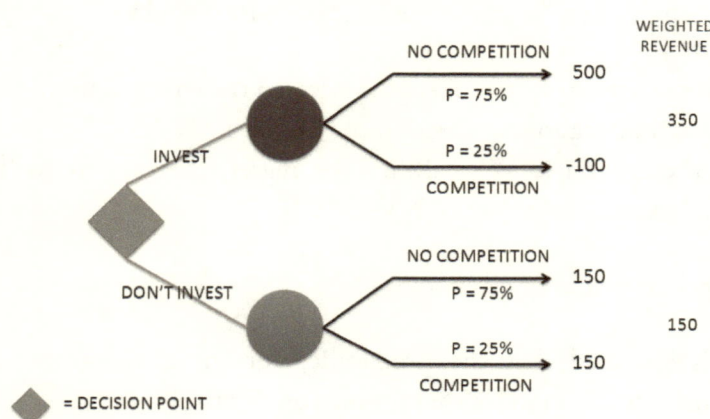

A second more detailed example is presented in the following document :

Document 17 – Decision tree – 2nd example

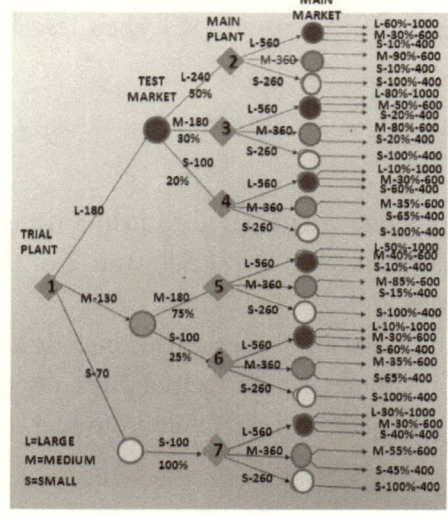

- 1ˢᵗ Decision :

    A decision must be made on investing in a pilot plant which would be either of Large size (L), medium size (M) or small size (S).

    Investment would be then :
    L : 180
    M : 130
    S : 70

    → If it is a Large pilot, the test market will lead to following discounted revenues with corresponding probabilities :

    240 for a Large market with 50% probability
    180 for a Medium market with 30% probability
    100 for a Small market with 20% probability

    → If it is a Medium pilot, the revenues from the market will be :

    180 for a Medium market with 75% probability
    100 for a Small market with 25% probability

    → If it is a Small pilot, the revenues from the market will be :

    100 for a small market with 100% probability

- 2ⁿᵈ Decision :

    A full size plant is then planned 2 years after, that could be :

    Large : Investment 560
    Medium : Investment 360
    Small : Investment 260

As for the pilot plant, the revenues from the market are indicated in the above decision tree, according to the probability affecting the market size.

The below calculation is providing the net cash-flow for each situation of the Decision No 2 (Decisions points No 2, 3, 4, 5, 6, 7). It is made by deducting the investment value from the respective revenues weighted by their probabilities.

The largest below calculated cash-flow is then 260, related to plant size L.

Then for each situation of the Decision No 1 (Pilot plant size), the corresponding revenues are added the discounted previous cash-flows and weighted with the test market probabilities.

The pilot plant corresponding investment value is then deducted and the analysis finally provides 3 discounted cumulated cash-flows related to the 3 different pilot sizes.

Conclusion : The largest value of these cumulated discounted cash-flows is 195, related to a pilot of a Medium size.

The global decision will be then to go for a M size pilot plant, followed by a L size full-size plant.

Note : The discount rate is 10%.

Document 18 – Criterion calculation from decision tree

Decision point			
2. L (1 000 × 0,6) + (600 × 0,3) + (400 × 0,1) = 560		260 *	
M (600 × 0,9) + (400 × 0,1) = 360		220	260
S (400 × 1,0) = 260		140	(L)
3. L (1 000 × 0,3) + (600 × 0,5) + (400 × 0,2) = 560		120	
M (600 × 0,8) + (400 × 0,2) = 360		200 *	200
S (400 × 1,0) = 260		140	(M)
4. L (1 000 × 0,1) + (600 × 0,3) + (400 × 0,6) = 560		40	
M (600 × 0,35) + (400 × 0,65) = 360		110	140
S (400 × 1,0) = 260		140 *	(S)
5. L (1 000 × 0,5) + (600 × 0,4) + (400 × 0,1) = 560		220 *	
M (600 × 0,85) + (400 × 0,15) = 360		210	220
S (400 × 1,0) = 260		140	(L)
6. L (1 000 × 0,1) + (600 × 0,3) + (400 × 0,6) = 560		40	
M (600 × 0,35) + (400 × 0,65) = 360		110	140
S (400 × 1,0) = 260		140 *	(S)
7. L (1 000 × 0,3) + (600 × 0,3) + (400 × 0,4) = 560		80	
M (600 × 0,55) + (400 × 0,45) = 360		150 *	150
S (400 × 1,0) = 260		140	(M)

$$1.\ L\ \left[\frac{260}{(1,1)^2} + 240\right] \times 0,5 + \left[\frac{200}{(1,1)^2} + 180\right] \times 0,3$$

$$+ \left[\frac{140}{(1,1)^2} + 100\right] \times 0,2 - 180 = 194$$

$$M\ \left[\frac{220}{(1,1)^2} + 180\right] \times 0,75 + \left[\frac{140}{(1,1)^2} + 100\right] \times 0,25 - 130 = 195\ *\quad 195\ (M)$$

$$S\ \left[\frac{150}{(1,1)^2} + 100\right] \times 1,0 - 70 = 154$$

5.2.6 Other methods

- Extreme values

  By this method, each parameter is given its minimum and maximum values, in order to get the extreme values of the resulting criteria.

It is however oftentimes giving too large ranges of variation of the criteria to be reasonably used for a conclusive decision. If the minimum value of the resulting range were to be selected, it would lead to a too conservative selection that would mask other opportunities.

Moreover, in case of a too high number of parameters, it is not likely that all their values could be simultaneously "low profile" ot "high profile".

- Minimum regrets (example above)
  It consists in analyzing each possible selection case, and evaluating or quantifying the regret to have not selected the alternatives, in the eventual case of a wrong selection.

  The final choice will be then the one leading to the minimum regret.

- Switching values
  It is the % change of a given parameter value for which the NPV falls to Zero. For instance, a 30% increase in the investment CAPEX would result in reducing NPV to Zero. Critical parameters and can be then studied one by one and listed, with the respective values of the change leading to NPV = 0.

5.3 Monte-Carlo analysis

5.3.1 Principles

Exogenous parameters are independent, by opposition to endogenous parameters, which values depend on parameters from the first category.

The probability laws of exogenous parameters can be estimated either from statistical observation, or from assumptions (subjective probabilities).

The aim is then to calculate from them the probability distribution of resulting endogenous parameters that represent economic or profitability criteria. The method consists in random picking a high number of exogenous parameters values according to their probability laws.

A distribution of the resulting endogenous parameters or needed criteria will then be obtained

5.3.2 Random numbers generation

It is possible to use random numbers tables, requiring time consuming way and back with intermediate files, or computer-based methods of "pseudo-random numbers" generation.

As on today, usual spreadsheets are providing built-in pseudo-random numbers generation.

5.3.3 Probability laws selection

The first step of the method is then to select a probability distribution law for each parameter, for which random values will be random picked according to that law.

Several standard distributions may be considered to reflect a subjective appreciation of the uncertainty, as presented below with typical graphs :

- Discrete distribution
  It consists in dividing the overall range of values into sub-ranges and to assign a probability to each sub-range. It is friendly, intuitive and usually providing fair results

  It becomes an approximation of the binomial law when the sampling is high, and is then a Poisson distribution.

Document 19 – Discrete distribution

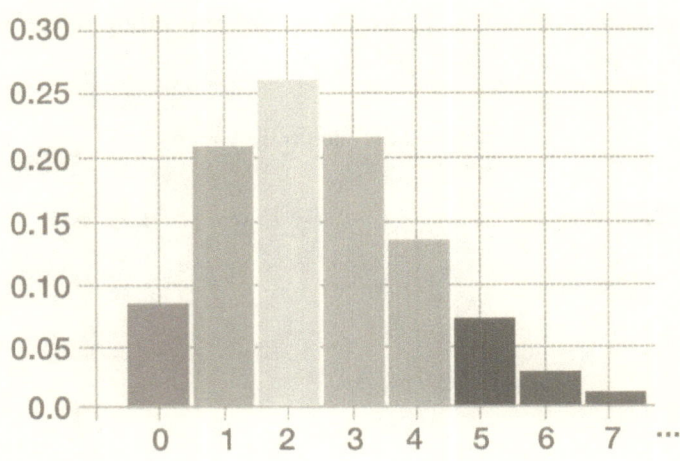

- Uniform distribution

  The below distribution reflects the difficulty in appreciating probability differences within the possible range of the values. It is not much realistic, as it supposes that a random parameter has equal chances to hit any value within the range, and 0 chances to be slightly lower or slightly higher.

  Document 20 – Uniform distribution

  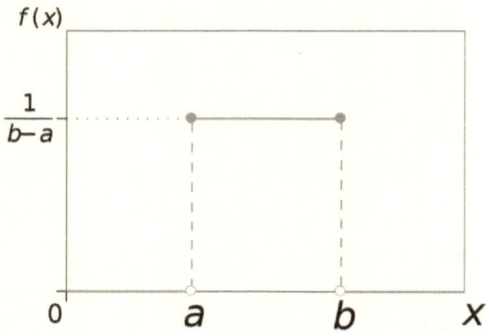

- Beta distribution

  The beta distribution is a family of continuous probability distributions characterized by two positive shape parameters, denoted by α and β, exponents of the random variable and control the shape of the distribution.

  Document 21 – Beta distribution

  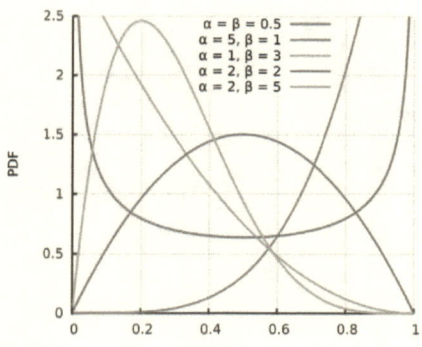

- Normal distribution
  This distribution is too regular and predictive to be adapted to a subjective appreciation of the uncertainty of a parameter.

  Document 22 – Normal distribution

  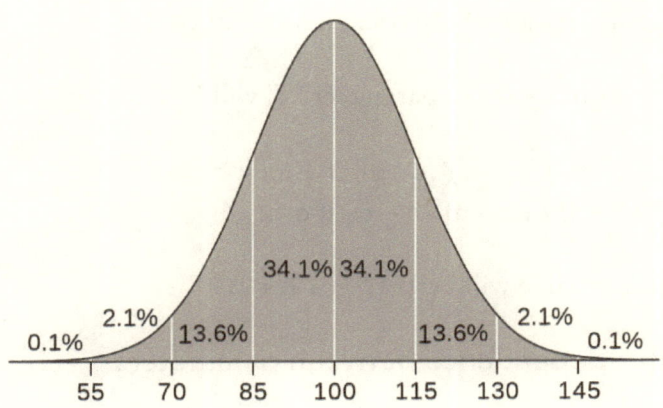

- Triangle distribution

  Document 23 – Triangle distribution

  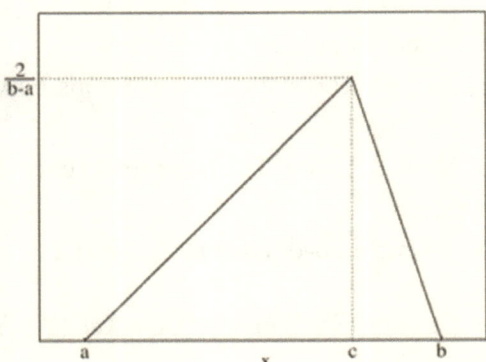

It is recognized that the results obtained from this type of (simple) distribution are close to those obtained from more sophisticated and refined distributions.

This distribution is "friendly" to non expert users, as the shape of the distribution can be obtained from the knowledge of :

- The minimum value "a", with a probability of 0
- The maximum value "c", with a probability of 0
- The value judged the most likely, with a probability equal to the normalization of the triangle area : 2/ (b – a)

The probability of the parameter "x" will be :

- $2*(x – a) / [(b – a)*(c – a)]$ if $a < x < c$
- $2*(b – x) / [(b – a)*(b – c)]$ if $c < x < b$

The mean value will be $1/3 * (a + b + c)$

5.3.4 Inter-dependence between parameters

In the case of 2 random parameters, their relative independence is not obvious and if inter-dependent, the nature of the correlation is not obvious either.

It is then possible to measure this correlation with the linear correlation coefficient "r" :

- If X and Y are two random parameters
- If SX and SY are the standard deviations between these two parameters
- If Xe and Ye or E(X) and E(Y), are the expected values of these two parameters
- If cov (X, Y) is the co-deviation of X and Y

Then $r = cov(X, Y) / (SX*SY) = E[(X – Xe)*(Y – Ye)] / (SX*SY)$

If $r = 1$ or if $r = -1$, the two parameters are inter-dependent.
If $r = 0$, the parameters are independent

In the reality, the value of "r" will comprised within the range [-1 ; 1]

Correlation between parameters is an important issue, and its evaluation will oftentimes have a higher impact than the probability law on the final simulations. For instance, if 2 parameters are acting in opposite ways on an economic criteria, and if they are inter-related or correlated, the effects of the variation of one of them will be compensated by the effects of the variations of the other. The probability to get extreme values of the criterion will then be lower than without correlation.

Oppositely, if two parameters are acting in the same way on a criteria, their correlation or inter-relation will lead to cumulate their effects, and the probability to get extreme values for the criterion will be higher than if they are independent.

There is no simple solution to this issue. The more parameters are disintegrated into their components, the easier to get the probability distribution of their components, and the smaller the uncertainties on these components. But on the other hand, the more parameters are disintegrated, the more correlations appear between their components.

If an initial parameter is disintegrated into N secondary components (which probability distributions are better known), the number of correlations to study is then 2**N.

The level of disintegration will then be subject to a careful evaluation.

5.3.5 Analysis of the simulation

The result of the Monte-Carlo simulation consists in a probability distribution of the criteria subject to the analysis.

The value of the probability "p" associated to the value of the criterion "r" is the probability that the criterion has a value lower than "r".

The median value of the criterion is the value having 50% to be obtained.

A high slope of the curve will mean a low dispersion of the possible values of the criterion, hence a lower uncertainty, or a lower risk.

The following document is displaying an example of the probability distribution of the NPV, from such a simulation. It says that the NPV has 10% probability to be lower than 1, or that it has 92% probability to be lower than 37.

Document 24 – NPV probability distribution from Monte-Carlo

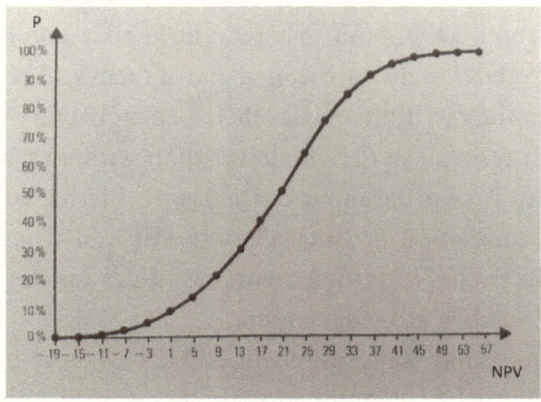

An Oracle software available in Excel 2016 and named "Crystal Ball" allows the user to perform such simulation on the basis of pre-defined probability distributions of the main parameters. The outcome will consist in graphs of above type and in usual statistics : sampling size, base case, mean, median, mode, standard deviation, variance etc...

The following graphs are displaying 2 situations when comparing investments

Document 25 – Comparison of 2 options – Case 1

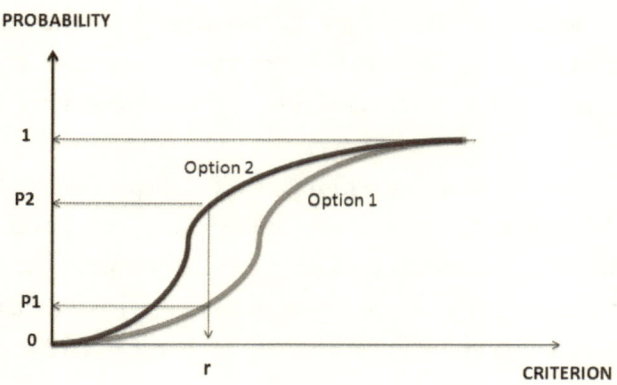

Document 26 – Comparison of 2 options – Case 2

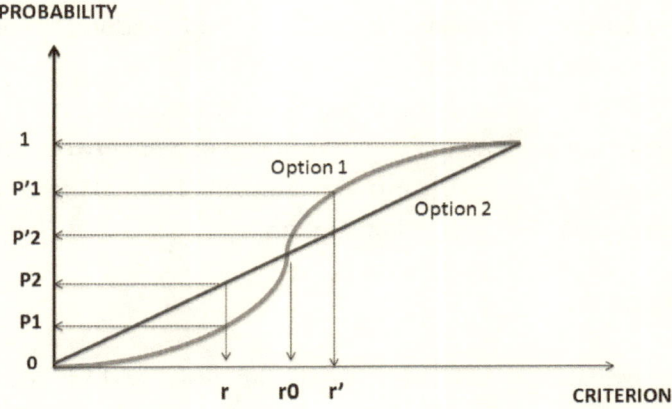

- In the Document 25, the probability distribution graph of the investment option 1 is below option 2 distribution for all possible values of the criterion.
  It means that the probability to get lower criterion value is always higher for option 2, thus that option 2 is less profitable than option 1.

- In the document 26, the 2 probability distributions are crossing each other at the value r0 of the criterion, for which both projects have the same profitability.
  The selection will depend on the "risk attitude" of the investor :

-Either he will minimize the probability of low criterion values and he will select the option 1.
-Or il will prioritize higher chances to have high values of the criterion against higher probability to get low values and he will select the option 2.

5.3.6 Influence of the random sampling size

This is the number of calculations of the criterion repeated by the computer on the basis of parameters generated random, according to their probability distributions.

For 300 calculations, the theorem of Kolmogorov states there is 95% probability for having a maximum gap of 8% between the "true" distribution (obtained with infinite number of calculations) and the distribution obtained with this sampling.

Conclusion :

The availability of Monte-Carlo analysis within commercial spreadsheets should contribute to spread this method among investors.

They must however use these simulations with caution, namely if the probability distributions of the main parameters are not based on sound historical data.

Sensitivity analysis on parameters distribution range must be conducted, and the results of the simulation must be compared to the results arising out of likely scenarii.

Last, to combine it with other methods is always recommended, before making a decision.

5.4 Global approach and flexibility : Real Options

The analysis of an investment in un-certain future, for instance from its NPV, assumes that a selection is made at some point in time, according to a "likely" scenario. Subsequent investment will be then implemented on an irreversible way.

In the reality, in such un-certain environment, the process of investment can be ended, put on hold, postponed, get modified, in order to catch late opportunities, benefit late market changes, adapt to a new technology or any future change...

The flexibility to switch to these "options" has a value in itself, that an investor should "combine' with the conventional NPV.

The value of an investment must be then supplemented by the value of its options.

The Real Options analysis can take into account certain options and determine their values, to be compared and combined to the conventional NPV of the selected and "likely" case investment.

For instance the value of the option "Defer the investment" (due to a new technology improvement) may be higher than the NPV of the selected basic investment.

As an option is seen as a strategic decision, this analysis will lead to the calculation of a "Strategic NPV", being the sum of the conventional NPV and the added value of the option.

Practically, the following options are the most commonly studied in such an analysis :

- Abandon (stop or sell the ongoing investment)
- Defer (delay the investment to benefit better times on capital market)
- Production flexibility (to modify production input/output to adapt to market)
- Stage investment (to invest step-by-step to adapt to market or technology)

As a conclusion, this fertile concept is still keeping the conventional NPV as an essential criteria of a "likely case" investment profitability, but complements and supplements it by the value of the flexibility to adapt it to changing conditions.

This guide is inviting the reader to refer to the article provided in the below Bibliography, for more details on the practical implementation.

CHAPTER 6

APPLICATION TO PRACTICAL CASES - SIMULATIONS

6.1 Industrial investment 87
    6.1.1 Investment on equities.. 88
    6.1.2 Investment with external financing........................ 89

6.2 Buy and rent out a property...91
    6.2.1 Buy on own funds 91
    6.2.2 Buy with mortgage and invest available funds on markets 92

6.3 Buy or Loan or Lease a car 94
    6.3.1 Buy on own funds 94
    6.3.2 Buy with a loan 95
    6.3.3 Leasing 96

6.4 Conclusions 99

CHAPTER 6

APPLICATION TO PRACTICAL CASES - SIMULATIONS

The prime objective of this guide is to provide practical guidelines and it is therefore coming along with a "companion website" offering detailed calculations for 3 practical cases that investors or buyers are typically dealing with.

The website address is :

https://www.investments-profitability-calculations-ericmatter.com

This registered website is providing the spreadsheets detailing the simulations related to the 3 profitability study cases.

The user will find there editable spreadsheets displaying the calculations and formulas of the study cases, and will be able to adapt them to his own situation, by modifying key parameters, such as discount rate, inflation rate, loans rates, average capital market return rate, taxation rate...

The user will also be able to conduct sensitivity analysis on main parameters, or build his own investment profile and case using these spreadsheet structures, or even improve the models by adding other parameters or risk analysis calculations.

It is reminded that a Monte-Carlo simulation module named "Crystal Ball" is available on Excel 2016. Therefore, the presented spreadsheets may be imported in that software version to benefit risk analysis as introduced in previous chapters.

The user will find 3 icons respectively representing an industrial investment, a real estate property acquisition and a car acquisition.

He will have to click on the associated Spreadsheet icon and the file will automatically open in his computer's spreadsheet software, in editable mode.

If the website is open from a smartphone, the file will have to be imported into an editable spreadsheet application.

The below documents, related to the results of every study case, are "screenshots" of the tables used in the respective spreadsheets.

6.1 Industrial investment

An investment is planned in a factory costing 300 MM $, supposed to be spent at Year 0. It will be depreciated at a 10% rate per year for 10 years.

Production sales and total production costs are amounting respectively 140 MM $ and 56 MM $ the first year, and are increasing in volumes by 2% every year (this increase assumption in volumes is not related to inflation).

It is assumed that the residual or cession value of the factory after the 10 years economic observation period, is 91 MM $.

Initial need in working capital is 10 MM $, and slightly fluctuates on the period.

Tax rate is set at 30% on profit for the case displayed, but remains adjustable for automatic re-calculation.

Inflation was set at 0%, 1% and 3%/y over the period, to study NPV sensitivity.

Loan interest rate is set at 3%, and is adjustable for re-calculation.

Discount rate is set at 5%, and is adjustable for re-calculation.

6.1.1 Investment on equities

The investment is entirely disbursed on equities (own funds) on Year 0.

Document 27 - STUDY CASE 1 : INDUSTRIAL INVESTMENT
1.1 INVESTMENT ON EQUITIES

MM$	Y0	Y1	Y2	Y3	Y4	Y5	Y6	Y7	Y8	Y9	Y10
Investment&resid.value	-300										91
Depreciation provision		-30	-30	-30	-30	-30	-30	-30	-30	-30	-30
Production sales		140	143	146	149	152	155	158	161	164	167
Production costs		-56	-58	-60	-61	-61	-62	-63	-64	-65	-66
Work capital variation		-10	-1	0	0	0	0	0	0	0	11
Tax		-16	-16	-17	-17	-18	-19	-19	-20	-21	-22
Cash-flow(profit +prov)	-300	58	67	69	71	72	74	75	77	79	182
Discounted cash-flow	-300	55	61	60	58	57	55	54	52	51	112
-------with inflation 1%	-300	56	62	61	60	59	58	57	56	55	123
Cumul disc.cash-flow	-300	-245	-184	-124	-66	-10	45	99	151	202	**314**
-------with inflation 1%	-300	-244	-182	-121	-60	-1	58	115	172	227	**350**

Discount rate	5%	Profitability criteria	No inflation	Inflation 1%	Inflation 3%
Inflation	1%	NPV	314	350	431.6
Loan interest	3%	IRR	20.5 %	21.5 %	24 %
Tax rate	30%	PAY-OUT TIME	5 years 2 m.	5 years	4 years 10 m.

The NPV calculated by cumulating the cash-flows discounted at a 5% rate, is 314 MM $ with no inflation, or in constant currency of Year 1.

The IRR, obtained by running the model to obtained NPV = 0, is 20.5 %

The pay-out time, time at which the cumulated discounted cash-flow is turning positive, is 5 years and 2 months.

The effect of inflation is quite clear on NPV, given then in current currency. An inflation of 1% per year for 10 years is inflating the NPV by 11%, from 314 to 350 MM $, while it increases the IRR from 20.5% to 21.5%. The effect on pay-out time is moderate, 2 months better out of 5 years.

The below graph is displaying the relation between NPV and discount rate for this study case, without and with 1% inflation.

IRR values in both situations are the discount rates for which NPV = 0.

Document 28 - STUDY CASE 1 : INDUSTRIAL INVESTMENT 1.1 INVESTMENT ON EQUITIES – Graph NPV vs Disc. Rate

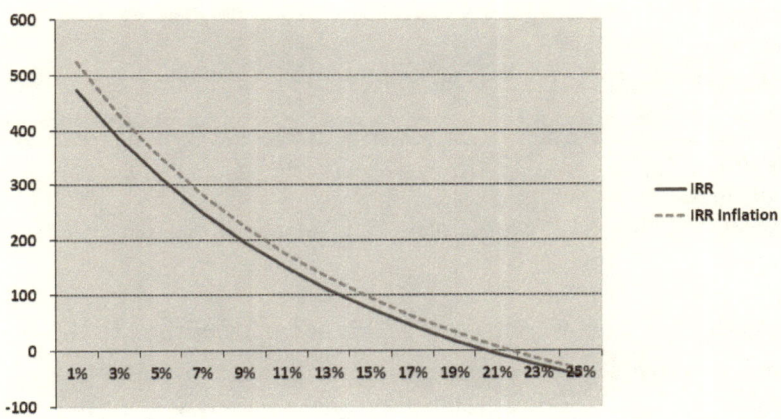

6.1.2 Investment with external financing

The same investment is made by financing 80% of its capital value at 3% interest rate, through a 10 years loan with constant repayment. Equities are then 20% of the investment, i.e. 60 MM $ out of 300 MM $.

Other parameters remain the same. It has been assumed that interests are deductible from taxable income.

Document 29 - STUDY CASE 1 : INDUSTRIAL INVESTMENT
1.2 INVESTMENT WITH 80% LOAN

MM$	Y0	Y1	Y2	Y3	Y4	Y5	Y6	Y7	Y8	Y9	Y10
Investment&resid value	-300										91
Loan draw & repay	240	-28	-28	-28	-28	-28	-28	-28	-28	-28	-28
Loan Interests		-6.9	-6.3	-5.6	-5	-4.3	-3.5	-2.8	-2	-1.3	-0.5
Tax saving on interest		2.1	1.9	1.7	1.5	1.3	1.1	0.8	0.6	0.4	0.2
Cash-flow	-60	32	41	43	44	45	47	48	49	51	154
Discounted cash-flow	-60	30	37	37	36	36	35	34	33	33	95
-------with inflation 1%	-60	31	39	39	39	38	38	38	38	38	106
Cumul disc.cash-flow	-60	-30	8	44	80	116	151	185	219	251	**346**
-------with inflation 1%	-60	-29	9	48	86	125	163	201	239	276	**383**

Discount rate	5%	Profitability criteria	No inflation	Inflation 1%	Inflation 3%
Inflation	1%	NPV	346	383	464
Loan interest	3%	RRE	65 %	67 %	72 %
Tax rate	30%	PAY-OUT TIME	1 year 10 m.	1 year 9 m.	1 year 8 m.

As the loan interest rate (here 3%) is much lower than IRR (20.5%), there is an obvious positive leverage effect of the loan, leading to a jump of the rate of return on equity (RRE = 65% compared to IRR = 20.5%)

The pay-out time is drastically reduced, as only 20% of the CAPEX is to be "recovered" by the investor through subsequent cash-flows.

The NPV increases in lower proportions (here by 10%, from 314 to 346), as the cash-flow is simultaneously loaded by the loan repayment.

6.2 Buy and rent out a property

Another study case is about investing in a property of 200 K$, to rent it out for 10 years and sell it back after 10 years at the market price, estimated at 300 K$. The rental revenues are slightly inflated yearly, through an assumption on the increase of rental price and owner's expenses of 1% per year.

Individual income tax is assumed at 20% on the profit of the rental activity.

Investor's discount rate is estimated at 2,5%. It is actually the average yearly return of his cash and savings (say bonds and life insurances).

6.2.1 Buy on own funds

Document 30 - STUDY CASE 2 : BUY & RENT OUT A PROPERTY
2.1 INVESTMENT ON OWN FUNDS

K$	Y0	Y1	Y2	Y3	Y4	Y5	Y6	Y7	Y8	Y9	Y10
House price & end value	-200										300
Rental revenues		12	12.1	12.2	12.4	12.5	12.6	12.7	12.9	13	13.1
Owner's expenses		-1	-1	-1	-1	-1	-1.1	-1.1	-1.1	-1.1	-1.1
Income tax		-2.2	-2.2	-2.2	-2.3	-2.3	-2.3	-2.3	-2.4	-2.4	-2.4
Cash-flow (profit – tax)	-200	8.8	8.9	9	9.1	9.1	9.2	9.3	9.4	9.5	310
Discounted cash-flow	-200	8.6	8.5	8.3	8.2	8.1	8	7.9	7.7	7.6	242
Cumul disc. cash-flow	-200	-191	-183	-175	-166	-158	-150	-142	-135	-127	115

Discount rate	2.5%	Profitability criteria	
Financial markets	5%	NPV	115
Loan interest	2.5%	IRR	8.1%
Income tax	20%	PAY-OUT TIME	9 years 6 m.
Rental increase/y	1%		

The above document is summarizing the main parameters and the outcome of the profitability criteria calculation :

- NPV is 115 K$ at the end of the economic observation
- IRR is 8.1%
- Pay-out time is 9 ½ years

The planned rental activity reveals then reasonably and steadily profitable, with however a relatively long pay-out time, by opposition of the previous investment study case. It shouldn't be a concern for this investor, as the risk of acquiring a real estate property is much lower than the risk carried by an industrial investment.

6.2.2 Buy with mortgage and invest available funds on markets

The same property is acquired through a loan (mortgage type at 2,5% interest rate) amounting 90% of the property price, and 10% on own funds.

The investor can then invest his remaining available funds (the 180 K$ borrowed to the bank) on the financial markets at an average return of 5% per year (Mix of bonds, insurances and stocks). The capital invested is assumed to be recovered the same at the end of the economic period.

Document 31 - STUDY CASE 2 : BUY & RENT OUT A HOUSE
2.2 BUY WITH MORTGAGE & INVEST AVAILABLE FUNDS

K$	Y0	Y1	Y2	Y3	Y4	Y5	Y6	Y7	Y8	Y9	Y10
House price & end value	-200										300
Loan draw & repaym.	180	-20.6	-20.6	-20.6	-20.6	-20.6	-20.6	-20.6	-20.6	-20.6	-20.6
Loan interests		-4.3	-4	-3.5	-3.1	-2.7	-2.2	-1.7	-1.2	-0.8	-0.3
Rental revenues		12	12.1	12.2	12.4	12.5	12.6	12.7	12.9	13	13.1
Owner's expenses		-1	-1	-1	-1	-1	-1.1	-1.1	-1.1	-1.1	-1.1
Income tax		-2.2	-2.2	-2.2	-2.3	-2.3	-2.3	-2.3	-2.4	-2.4	-2.4
Invested amount	-180										180
Return from markets		9	9.5	9.9	10.4	10.9	11.5	12.1	12.7	13.3	14
Cash-flow (profit − tax)	-200	-1.9	-1.4	-1	-0.5	0.1	0.6	1.2	1.8	2.4	483
Discounted cash-flow	-200	-1.9	-1.4	-0.9	-0.4	0.1	0.5	1	1.5	1.9	377
Cumul disc. cash-flow	-200	-202	-203	-204	-205	-204	-204	-203	-202	-200	**178**

Discount rate	2.5%	Profitability criteria	
Financial markets	5%	NPV	178
Loan interest	2.5%	RRE	9.2 %
Income tax	20%	PAY-OUT TIME	9 years 5 m.

The loan interest rate being lower than the IRR (previously calculated), there is a positive leverage on the overall profitability, for which :

- NPV climbs to 178 K$ (compared to 115 on own funds investment)
- RRE raises to 9.2%
- Pay-out time is slightly shortened by a month

From the standpoint of such a private investor, the NPV is definitely the most important criteria for a decision, as it expresses the tangible funds he will earn.

Such low risk investment does not require a short pay-out time, and the IRR or RRE values are not as important as they are in a corporate reporting.

6.3 Buy or Loan or Lease a car

Another study case related to the everyday life of an individual consumer is to study the best option for acquiring a car, among the following :

- Buying the car on own funds
- Using a conventional loan (and invest the available fund on markets)
- Leasing the car (and invest the available fund on markets)

Note : This case is studying the economics of an expense with no revenues.

6.3.1 Buy on own funds

The car cost is 52 K$ and has a residual value of 10 K$ after 8 years. Maintenance costs are assumed to be nil for the 4 first years and 1 K$ per year for the 4 following years.

The discount rate of the buyer is still 2.5 % per year.

**Document 32 - STUDY CASE 3 : BUY OR LOAN OR LEASE A CAR
3.1 BUY ON OWN FUNDS**

K$	Y0	Y1	Y2	Y3	Y4	Y5	Y6	Y7	Y8
Car price & end value	-52								10
Maintenance costs		0	0	0	0	-1	-1	-1	-1
Cash-flow	-52	0	0	0	0	-1	-1	-1	9
Discounted cash-flow	-52	0	0	0	0	-0.9	-0.9	-0.8	7.4
Cumul disc.cash-flow	-52	-52	-52	-52	-52	-53	-54	-55	-47

Discount rate	2.5%	Profitability criteria	Y8 value=10	Y8 value=7	Y8 value=13
Financial markets	5%	NPV	-47	-50	-45
Loan interest	4%	IRR	-	-	-
Income tax	20%	PAY-OUT TIME	-	-	-

The NPV is – 47 K$ for a residual value of 10 K$.

A sensitivity on the residual value after 8 years shows that NPV varies within a range [- 50 ; - 45] for residual values comprised within [7 K$; 13 K$].

IRR and pay-out time have no meaning as there are no revenues to balance the initial disbursement.

6.3.2 Buy with a loan

The same car is acquired through a loan of 44 K$ over 8 years at 4% interest rate, and 8 K$ on own funds, while the (now available) 44 K$ funds are invested on financial markets at 5% average return rate. As for the previous case, the invested amount is recovered the same after 8 years, for the sake of getting conservative results.

Document 33 - STUDY CASE 3 : BUY OR LOAN OR LEASE A CAR
3.2 LOAN & INVEST AVAILABLE FUND

K$	Y0	Y1	Y2	Y3	Y4	Y5	Y6	Y7	Y8
Car price & end value	-52								10
Loan draw & repaym.	44	-6.5	-6.5	-6.5	-6.5	-6.5	-6.5	-6.5	-6.5
Maintenance costs		0	0	0	0	-1	-1	-1	-1
Financial market invest	-44								44
Financial market return		2.2	2.3	2.4	2.5	2.7	2.8	2.9	3.1
Cash-flow	-52	-4.3	-4.2	-4.1	-4	-4.9	-4.7	-4.6	50
Discounted cash-flow	-52	-4.2	-4	-3.8	-3.6	-4.3	-4.1	-3.9	41
Cumul disc.cash-flow	-52	-56	-60	-64	-68	-72	-76	-80	**-39**

Discount rate	2.5%	Profitability criteria	Y8 value=10	Y8 value=7	Y8 value=13
Financial markets	5%	NPV	-39	-42	-37
Loan interest	4%	IRR	-	-	-
Income tax	20%	PAY-OUT TIME	-	-	-

The NPV is – 39 K$ and varies within a range [- 42 ; - 37] for residual values comprised within [7 K$; 13 K$].

NPV is thus algebraically higher than for the acquisition on own funds.

It means that the option of borrowing (at 4% rate) and investing the available funds (at 5% return rate) is economically more favorable than buying the car on own cash, and allows savings of about 20% in NPV.

Notes :

- *A simulation made by reducing the investment return rate from 5% to 4% shows that the economic advantage over cash option is reduced from the above 20% NPV savings to about 10% NPV savings. -A simulation made by taking the same rate for discount rate, loan interest and investment return rate (say 4%) shows that the effect of borrowing is neutralized compared to buying the car on cash.*

6.3.3 Leasing

The 3rd option is to proceed with 2 consecutive leasing periods of 4 years each, for 2 identical cars, assuming that the 2nd car price (and related amounts) is 10% higher after 4 years.

The down payment for each leasing is proportionally the same than for the previous loan option (8 K$ for the first 52 K$ car leasing, 8 K$ + 10% = 8.8 K$ for the second car leasing).

The residual value of the first car is assumed to be 32 K$ after 4 years, and the residual value of the second car (acquired at the end of Year 4) is then 32 K$ + 10% = 35 K$ at the end of Year 8.

The leasing contractual last payment is set at 25 K$ for the first car, and at 25 + 10% = 28 K$ for the second car.

Note : The leasing data have been taken from an actual leasing proposal provided by a car maker offering a car of a 52 K$ value.

As for the previous loan option, the initial available fund of 44 K$ is invested on the financial market for 8 years at the same return rate of 5% per year, and recovered the same after the 8 years.

Document 34 - STUDY CASE 3 : BUY OR LOAN OR LEASE A CAR
3.3 LEASE & INVEST AVAILABLE FUND

K$	Y0	Y1	Y2	Y3	Y4	Y5	Y6	Y7	Y8
1st car Dpaym. & end value	-8				32				
1st Leasing repayment		-6.1	-6.1	-6.1	-6.1				
Leasing last payment					-25				
2nd car Dpaym. & end value					-8.8				35
2nd Leasing repayment						-6.7	-6.7	-6.7	-6.7
Leasing last payment									-28
Financial market invest/ret	-44	2.2	2.3	2.4	2.5	2.7	2.8	2.9	3.1+44
Cash-flow	-52	-3.9	-3.8	-3.7	-5.4	-4	-3.9	-3.8	48
Discounted cash-flow	-52	-3.8	-3.6	-3.4	-4.8	-3.6	-3.4	-3.2	40
Cumul disc.cash-flow	-52	-56	-59	-63	-68	-71	-75	-78	**-38**

Discount rate	2.5%	Profitability	Y4 value=32	Y4 value=29	Y4 value=35
Financial markets	5%	NPV	-38	-44	-33
Loan interest	4%	IRR	-	-	-
Income tax	20%	PAY-OUT TIME	-	-	-

The NPV obtained is – 38 K$, i.e. slightly above the NPV obtained in the previous loan option with the same basic data. Given the uncertainty of some parameters (e.g. residual value), we will consider that the NPV is about the same than for loan option.

NPV sensitivity to the residual value after 4 years is quite high. NPV varies within a range [- 44 K$; - 33 K$] for a residual value ranging within [29 K$; 35 K$]

The following document is displaying the NPV ranges versus residual value ranges for the 3 options, and shows that the loan and leasing options are both better economic options than the cash option.

Document 35 - STUDY CASE 3 : BUY OR LOAN OR LEASE A CAR PROFITABILITY RANGE vs CAR RESIDUAL VALUE RANGE

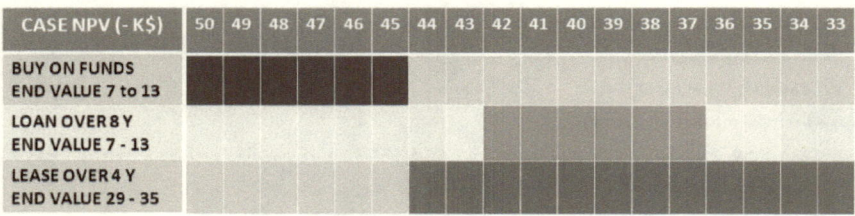

These results may be judged intuitively obvious, however the simulation models provided in the companion website are providing a reasonable quantification on the basis of all main parameters, that the user can adapt to his own situation.

As a last remark on the risk standpoint, an external financing of the acquisition of an asset (industrial plant, property, car...) is not only to be seen as a way to improve economics and release own resources (that we can invest elsewhere), but also as a way to partly transfer the global risk, or certain liabilities, to the financing entity.

Such assets will depreciate, may get damaged, lost or not fulfilling their function, or become obsolete to the market... In these situations, the financing entity and their insurances will bear most of the immediate consequences, while the risk of the investor will remain limited to the equities he has invested.

6.4 Conclusions

The above study cases are meant to show how to build discounted cash-flow tables and deduct from them the main profitability criteria, such as NPV, IRR, RRE, Pay-out time.

They offer the possibility to study the sensitivity of these criteria to such parameters like discount rate, inflation rate, financing interest rate, tax rate, financial markets (simple) return rate, residual value…

The simulation models can however be improved by :

- Offering different loan modes (capital straight line and mortgage)
- Offering different depreciation modes
- Allowing an Investment period during x years instead of a punctual investment at Year Zero
- Offering loan interest capitalization during investment period
- Offering taxation grace periods and losses carry forward
- Offering a non flat inflation profile over the duration
- Breaking down costs into production rate, raw materials unit prices, products unit prices, variable costs, fixed costs.….
- Offering at least 2 currencies (local and foreign) with change rate.
- Graphs generation

The reader of this guide is then encouraged to implement these improvements for the purpose of training, or customize the provided simulations as per his needs.

It is also suggested to the reader to supplement the provided simulations with a risk analysis module, for instance by adding Monte-Carlo built-in module available on Excel version 2016.

The reader will find a dialog box in the companion website, where he will be allowed to send questions, comments and suggestions.

CHAPTER 7

PROFITABILITY OF PUBLIC INVESTMENTS

7.1 Introduction 103
7.2 Economic appraisal Methodologies 104
    7.2.1 Cost-Benefit Analysis (CBA) 105
    7.2.2 Cost-Effectiveness Analysis (CEA) 105
    7.2.3 Multi-Criteria Analysis (MCA) 105
    7.2.4 Comparative suitability of the economic appraisal methodologies 106
7.3 Double-Scoring Methodology 107
7.4 Distribution analysis 107

7.1 Introduction

Private investments selection are based on the evaluation of certain profitability criteria, as presented above.

This methodology is centered around the quantification of profit, and is insufficient for public investments and projects.

Other dimensions have to be taken into account :

- National priorities and objectives
- Social benefits and welfare
- Macro-economy
- Sustainable growth of communities,

with a permanent focus on future uncertainty and avoidance of critical risks.

It may happen for instance that for certain public investments, there may be no financial return from the investor standpoint (e.g. facility offered free of charge), but great social benefits from the users standpoint.

There are specific methodologies to evaluate intangible costs and benefits, and select such investments.

This guide does not aim to provide details on these methodologies, but to summarize their principles and show emphasis on the differences between private investments and public spending selection criteria.

7.2 Economic appraisal Methodologies

The below elements are summarizing the policies of the European Investment Bank and are applied by number of other countries.

Beside the *financial appraisals* prevailing in the private sector, decisions of Public Institutional banks are rather driven by *economic appraisals,* including all benefits and costs to the society and evaluating the value generated to all participants involved in the *investment* to select (The Institutional Investor, the country, the communities, the environment…).

The economic appraisal does not replace the financial appraisal, but complements it.

It takes into account external costs and benefits coming as a consequence of an investment, such as the impact of an infrastructure to users (time savings), to public safety, to environment and pollution etc…

Another application of an economic appraisal (versus the sole financial appraisal) is to evaluate the global impact of taxes and subsidies on a given investment : the investor will evaluate it as profitable because of tax reductions or incentives, but the government will suffer a revenue loss and the consumers may consequently suffer taxes rises.

Reversely, an incentive may be provided to the consumer of such investment output, through a distortion of the market price, which may affect the profitability from the Investor standpoint, but will result in benefits for the citizens.

Due to such distortions, economic values (for the society) of investment's input and output may be different from their financial market values.

Below methodologies are complementing financial analysis, and lead to a broader appraisal of ability to meet public needs and costs/benefits to society.

7.2.1 Cost-Benefit Analysis (CBA)

This methodology was originated in Europe long ago and became a standard method to assess the socio-economic justification of a public investment.

Its principle is to compare the social/economic costs of a public investment to its social/economic benefits. Benefits shall of course exceed costs.

CBA consists in measuring the difference between all costs and benefits (direct and indirect) when there is an Investment – or related options – and all costs and benefits if no Investment. The analysis is generally running on very long periods, at the scale of infrastructures lifetime.

The analysis is resulting in an *Economic Rate of Return* (ERR) and an *Economic Net Present Value* (ENPV).

The investment is sanctioned if the ERR is exceeding the "social" discount rate and if the ENPV is positive.

7.2.2 Cost-Effectiveness Analysis (CEA)

Should a detailed CBA reveal difficult to conduct due to the unavailability of data, or because certain benefits are not easy to quantify, the Investor may proceed to a CEA.

It consists in evaluating the cost of reaching a certain target (e.g. the production level or an infrastructure size…), for instance when different technologies are competing to lead to the said target.

The selected option is then the one providing the highest output per unit of input (for instance the highest production per unit of consumed energy).

7.2.3 Multi-Criteria Analysis (MCA)

It is applied when the 2 above methods are not practical. It combines different evaluations (having their own criteria) in weighting them into a single "score", that will be used to compare different options.

It doesn't focus only on financial or tangible appraisal. Above evaluation criteria can be typically :

- Income distribution
- Compliance with nation's objectives
- Quality
- Visual appearance
- Others

7.2.4 Comparative suitability of the economic appraisal methodologies

The below table is comparing the suitability of these methodologies, depending on the number of resulting criteria to study, and their ability to be easily measurable and monetized :

METHODOLOGY SUITABILITY	**High** Nb of resulting criteria	**Low** Nb of resulting criteria
Resulting criteria EASY measurability & monetization	**CBA & CEA**	**CBA & CEA**
Resulting criteria DIFFICULT measurability & monetization	**MCA**	**CEA**

The use of these methodologies is also depending on the Public Sector it relates to :

CBA	CEA	MCA
Agro-Industry	Energy	Education
Energy	Waste management	Healthcare
Manufacturing	Education	Urban Development
Telecoms	Healthcare	Public services
Tourism		
Transport		

7.3 Double-Scoring Methodology

This methodology has been tested by United Nations Development program in Kuwait.

It requires 2 scoring tables :

- The national priorities, ranked by their importance (for instance : social progress, economic growth, urban development, health, cost-efficiency, agriculture, infrastructures, science, education, defence, competitiveness…)
- The Investments forecast for the fiscal year, scored by their level of compliance to each national priority.

The investments are then finally ranked as per a global score, and the selection is operated by taking the best ranking projects up to the value of the agreed budget.

7.4 Distribution analysis

Usual NPV calculation do not consider the distribution of costs and benefits among different groups of the society (by income, gender, age, geographical location…), while there may be different impacts according to the distribution of society within these groups.

The investor may then study the impact of a public investment on a partition of groups having different income, age etc… Weights are affected to the groups according to national policies or priorities, and a weighted impact criteria can be built to select different options.

APPENDICES

Appendix 3 Dedicated Companion Web Site.................................. 111

Appendix 4 Summary of Useful Formulas 117

APPENDIX 1

DEDICATED COMPANION WEB SITE

The website address is :
https://www.investments-profitability-calculations-ericmatter.com

It is providing spreadsheets detailing the simulations of 3 profitability study cases.

The user will find hereby editable spreadsheets displaying the calculations and formulas of the study cases, and will be able to adapt them to his own situation.

The user will find 3 icons respectively representing an industrial investment, a real estate property acquisition and a car acquisition. He will have to click on the associated Spreadsheet icon and the file will automatically open in his computer's spreadsheet software, in editable mode.

If the website is open from a smartphone, the file will open by clicking on the spreadsheet icon, and will have to be imported into an editable spreadsheet application.

The appearance of its home page on a smartphone is shown on below screenshots :

INVESTMENTS
PROFITABILITY
ANALYSIS
STUDY CASES FOR
INDUSTRIAL AND
PRIVATE USERS

PROFITABILITY CRITERIA CALCULATIONS. STUDY CASES SPREADSHEETS

Open below files icons using Excel on a computer.
Or open and copy/paste the table template on a spreadsheet App, from a smartphone

STUDY CASE 1 : INDUSTRIAL INVESTMENT SELECTION & PROFITABILITY

STUDY CASE 2 : PROPERTY INVESTMENT, OWN FUNDS OR MORTGAGE

STUDY CASE 3 : COST EFFECTIVENESS FOR BUY, LOAN OR LEASE A CAR

A dialog box located at the bottom of the home page is allowing the user to send comments or questions.

APPENDIX 2

SUMMARY OF USEFUL FORMULAS

Although commonly-used formulas are "built-in" within the most popular spreadsheets, they are reminded here below.

Note on symbols used in this guide :

"*" means "multiply by" (for instance 3 * 2 = 6)
"**" means "power" (for instance 3 ** 2 = 9)

2.1 Mortgage loans

$M = L * [i (1 + i)**n] / [(1 + i)**n - 1]$, whereby :

M = Monthly payment
L = Loan amount
i = Interest rate
n = Number of monthly payments

2.2 Investment through Compound interests

$C = I * [(1 + i/n)**(n*t)]$, whereby :

C = Future value of the Investment at the end of the period
I = Initial amount invested
i = Interest rate
n = Number of times that interest is compounded per year
t = Number of years of investment

2.3 Compound interest back calculation

$i = (C / I)**(1/t) - 1$, whereby :

C = future value of the capital obtained after t years
I = Initial investment

2.4 Investment Duration back calculation

$t = [Ln(C / I)] / [Ln(1 + i)]$, whereby :

t is the required number of years to get a capital C from an initiatial investment I, given an interest i.

Note : "Ln" is natural logarithm

BIBLIOGRAPHY

- *"The parameter method for risk analysis"*, D.O. Cooper, L.B. Davidson
- "Uncertainty analysis helps in making business decisions, R.C. Ross
- *"Risk evaluation helps making better decisions"*, P.D. Newendorp
- *"Investigating project profitability in case of uncertain returns : a simulation approach"*, Goran Avlijas & Vule Mizdrakovic, Singidunum University, Belgrade, Serbia
- *"Assessment of Investment Project Profitability in Uncertain Environment : a Real Option Approach"*, Jihane Gharib, Mohammed V University, Rabat, Morocco
- *"The Economic Appraisal of Investment Projects at the EIB"*, J. Doramas Jorge-Calderon, Harald Gruber & Pierre-Etienne Bouchaud, European Investment Bank
- *"Public Project Evaluation and Selection"*, Alex Mosesova & Sudhakar Kota, Skyline College, Sharjah, UAE
- *"The Public Spending Code : D. Standard Analytical Procedures – Overview of Appraisal Methods and Techniques"*, Irish Government Economic & Evaluation Service

www.ingramcontent.com/pod-product-compliance
Lightning Source LLC
Chambersburg PA
CBHW030814180526
45163CB00003B/1283